What people are saying about
Leadership in a Challenging World . . .

"This is a moving story of personal discovery—discovery of what leadership means in today's business world. Barbara Shipka's "eight powers" comprise an easily remembered yet profoundly inclusive mantra for invoking one's true ability to lead—in the broadest possible sense."

—WILLIS HARMAN, PRESIDENT, THE INSTITUTE OF NOETIC SCIENCES

"A new and comprehensive guide to the really challenging issues and personal responsibilities of leading any organization."

—HAZEL HENDERSON
Paradigms in Progress and *Building a Win-Win World*

"This book has a simple but challenging premise: to fundamentally change business, each person must come to see their life as a story that in large measure is told through their personal growth and its impact on business practice. It has an amazing unity of emotional, intellectual, and spiritual life which is told with such honesty that makes it compelling and unforgettable."

—F. BYRON NAHSER, PRESIDENT & CEO, NAHSER ADVERTISING
Learning to Read the Signs: Reclaiming Pragmatism in Business

"Most business books are written one dimensionally and often convey an intellectual viewpoint without linking it to the heart. What I love about Barbara's book is that she conveys deep feeling in her brilliant ability at storytelling and then moves into concrete examples of what it means to be sustainable in business today."

—JACQUELINE CAMBATA, CEO, PHOENIX CHEMICAL LIMITED

Leadership in a Challenging World

Leadership in a Challenging World: A Sacred Journey

by
Barbara Shipka

Illustrations by
Margi Orman

Butterworth–Heinemann

Boston   Oxford   Johannesburg   Melbourne
          New Delhi   Singapore

Illustrations by Margaret E. Orman, Copyright© 1996.

Willowheart logo copyright© 1988 by Barbara Jo Shipka.
Original design by Paul Abdella.

Excerpt from *Truth or Dare* by Starhawk. Copyright© 1987 by Miriam Simos.
Reprinted by permission of HarperCollins Publishers, Inc.

Recognizing the importance of preserving what has been written,
Butterworth–Heinemann prints its books on acid-free paper
whenever possible.

Library of Congress Cataloging-in-Publication Data

Shipka, Barbara
    Leadership in a challenging world: a sacred journey/by Barbara Shipka:
illustrations by Margi Orman.
       p. cm.
    ISBN 0-7506-9750-4 (pbk.)
     1. Leadership. 2. Management. I. Title.
    HD57. 7. S493 1996
    658. 4' 092—dc20   96-24390

                                          CIP

British Library Cataloguing-in-Publication Data

A catalogue record for this book is available from the British Library.

The publisher offers special discounts on bulk orders of this book.

For information, please contact:
Manager of Special Sales
Butterworth–Heinemann
313 Washington Street
Newton, MA 02158–1626
Tel: 617-928-2500
Fax: 617-928-2620

For information on all business publications available, contact our World Wide Web
home page at: http://www.bh.com/bh/bb

10 9 8 7 6 5 4 3 2 1

Printed in the United States of America

Hear the story woman

She says…

There are times, sisters and brothers

when we are afraid that we will die

and take the whole great humming dance of life with us

Something must change, we know that

But are we strong enough?

And will we be given time?…

When we are afraid, when it hurts too much

We like to tell ourselves

stories of power

how we lost it

how we can reclaim it

We tell ourselves

the cries we hear may be those of labor

the pain we feel may yet be that of birth

—excerpted from "A Story of Beginnings" *in Truth or Dare*

BY STARHAWK

Dedication

For the children

We have not inherited the earth from our ancestors. We have only borrowed it from our children.

—Ancient Proverb

Table of Contents

The Forest II: Envisioning Possibilities

Part II: A Path

A Path I: Walking Within

List of Illustrations

Acknowledgments

To Cathy Yandell, Michele Smith, Jan Dolejsi, and Charlaine Tolkien for planting the seed of possibility in my mind when they each, independently, urged me to write.

To Peter Krembs, Cheryl Alexander, Christina Baldwin, Charlaine Tolkien, Sarita Chawla, and Kazimierz Gozdz for nurturing by watering and tending the young shoot through their gifts of hours of reading, critique, and cheerleading of my previous writing. To Magaly Rodriguez for suggesting—once when I was stuck—that I hold the world's children in my mind and heart and write to and for *them*. To John Renesch for creating the garden in which the seed could be planted through the New Leaders Press Business Anthologies.

To Susen Fagrelius, Pablo Gaito, Peter Krembs, Jeff Linzer, Vijit Ramchandani, Jan Smith, and Karen Speerstra who have been consciously tending the plant as it grows into its first season of blossom. They committed to sit together in dialogue periodicially to support my writing process; they gave invaluable feedback on the first draft; and they have been present for me as I wrote. Without them this plant may have died from drought or frostbite. Additionally, to Nancy Cosgriff, Jan Dolejsi, Margaret Lulic, and Lesley and Terrence Taylor for the generous gift of their time and feedback in reading the first draft.

To Karen Speerstra whose skill at gardening is great and whose skill at midwifery is even greater. Through her work of publishing books on themes of spirituality and transformation in business she is assisting in the birth of new potential.

To Margi Orman for her ability to capture on paper the images in my mind with class and simplicity.

To clients past and present, for offering me an incredible milieu in which to learn, create, and grow. It happens best and most when we do it together.

To John Adams and Sabina Spencer for introducing me to the World Business Academy; and to the many wonderful passionate, committed and visionary people I have the privilege to know and have come to love as a result.

To those on the homefront who give love and support to Michael and me—and who cared for us in tender and unique ways during this project: Cheryl Beardslee, Jody, Doug, and Shawn Carlson, Dinesh Chandra, Steve Figlmiller, Aaron Flickstein, Carol Frenier, Peter Krembs, Sharon Lehrer, Margaret Lulic, Ricka and Josh Kohnstamm, Jeff Linzer, Alec, Cary, Patricia, and Craig Neal, Patty and Bill Thomson, Rosie and Peter Sam.

To *all* of you who form the past, current, and potential mosaic of of relatedness and connectedness that is my life. In an ever-present rush to meet a deadline, I may have regretfully forgotten to *mention* you, but I have not forgotten you.

And most of all to my son, Michael, who is my most demanding and rewarding teacher. Each day I wrote he called me back out of the book and into our routine. He helped maintain the balance, the bliss—and, now and then, the blasphemy—of the "real world."

Thank you all for the ways in which we co-create together. I am indeed grateful to walk with you for a time on planet Earth.

Preface

The Forest and a Path

The present-day global landscape is one of profound crisis, which could end either in the death of humankind or in the breakthrough to a new civilization... It is up to all of us who live today on this planet...

—MIKHAIL GORBACHEV

About the Forest and a Path
Why I Wrote this Book
Why You Might Want to Read It
A Brief "Field Guide" of Words

About the Forest and a Path

Part I of this book is a look at the forest. A forest is more than trees; it is a whole system. It includes the rain that falls, the squirrels that chatter, the birds' morning song, the sun shining on the leaves, the mushrooms popping out of a dead tree trunk, the cool, fresh air, the waterfall. A forest is the setting, the context, through which we walk. Within it the entire cycle of birth, growth, and death is taking place continuously. So it is with our world. The world is our forest, our context.

A forest holds danger and enchantment at the same time. "The Forest I: Demanding Challenges" is a broad-brush look into the trends that are threatening the weather and the wild animals of the forest that is our world. It has elements of despair and loss for what is apparently dying.

"The Forest II: Envisioning Possibilities" looks with hope toward what might be born, indeed what is being born, through the potential of the creative, generative life-force in general, and human ingenuity and imagination specifically.

Part II of the book is a walk on one path through the forest. When you are hiking, the whole forest itself is the destination; the walk itself is the purpose. You may have the goal of reaching a waterfall, a lake, or a lighthouse; but the true final destination is usually to return to where you began. So it is with your walk through life. Awareness of the walk itself, of being on a path, is its own destination. Walking day in and day out, you come to know more and more about your chosen path—and about your own nature as well. Through the practice of walking you find yourself developing strength, resilience, and peace. One day you notice that you are moving into greater harmony with the entire forest—just by walking along the path.

The true final destination is usually to return to where you began.

Your entire life is a path through the forest. The path in this book is about further developing eight powers you already have for your journey of leadership. It is an often-used path that has been tended, explored, and traveled, for millennia—by many people the world over.

Why I Wrote this Book

All people, throughout all of human experience, have witnessed the cycle of birth, growth, and death, both of themselves and of life in the forest around them. But not all people have lived in a time when it appears that the entire forest may die and leave the ground barren. You and I live during such a time.

By virtue of its infrastructure, resources, and power in the world today, business directly determines what dies, and what is born; how much dies, and how much is born; and the quality of growth and life experienced in between. Business has a critical role to play in the future of the forest, whether or not people within it are conscious of that reality—and the responsibility it entails. Business is a major force in determining the future of all life as we know it. And, in truth, like any other institution, "business," is merely a set of agreements people have made, maintain, or change over time. In other words, business is you, me, and everyone else that takes part, however indirectly, in the arrangements that make our economy work. This means our leadership is critical—and a big responsibility.

In 1986, having spent the previous three years working with the United Nations High Commission for Refugees in Somalia, The Sudan, and Ethiopia, I reached a watershed in my career: to accept a position working with the World Bank in Papua New

Guinea, and make international development work my path; or to return to corporate America and the consulting practice that I had left in suspension.

I leaned toward international development work; there is so much to do in the world, and the opportunity to make a difference seemed so great. But an incident in my life that occurred around that time continually entered my mind.

I was spending the morning with a monk of the Ethiopian Catholic Church in Asmara, who managed food distribution for the region. In his office was a chalkboard with a grid drawn on it. Down the left side were the names of villages; across the top were the months of the year. The boxes within the grid held numbers like "10,000," "20,000," and "40,000." The brother explained, "This graph reflects the amount of food we distribute."

It was February. I noticed that from April onward many of the boxes had a simple, stark "X" drawn through them. I asked the monk about these. He explained, "Beginning in April the Poles will take back the helicopters they have lent us. They need them for other purposes. The villages with X's through their boxes," he went on, "can only be reached by air." I felt breathless. "What will happen?" I asked. "Those people have no more food, and no more ability to get food, than they did before, have they?" "No, they haven't," he responded. "But the world's attention has shifted; many people think the drought and famine have passed."

In this situation, when food stopped arriving, people walked or died—or walked *and* died. In my work in Africa, we treated symptoms, one after another; but little fundamentally changed. Unless and until the systems change, people die. Reflecting on my encounter with the monk I too wondered: What systems, if altered, could make a difference in the world? I chose to return to my consulting practice in corporate business. I felt a twinge of self-indulgence, returning to an easier daily life. Mentioning my concern that I was "copping out" to my friend Michael, he replied, "Let's get honest here. Do you really find working in corporate America to be easy? It's tough. And critical. It's possible that if business doesn't make it, none of us will."

> *When we change our minds, our agreements, and our*
> *practices, systems change.*

"Making it" means more than succeeding in conventional terms. It means succeeding while changing dramatically by altering organization and global systems to support the viability of the forest, our world. How are such systems altered? Through you and me and how we think about ourselves and our relationship to the world. When we change our minds, our agreements, and our practices, systems change.

To change our minds we must go deep; both deep into the forest, and deep into ourselves as we walk the path. Some days you can easily see a distance along the way because there's less fog; sometimes you have to bushwhack your way around a fallen tree or ford a brook. Persistence and resourcefulness, and even a walking stick, help at those times. This book is a walking stick to support your walk on the path of your life's work — the work of providing leadership in the business world during times of enormous change and transition. These are times in which your journey requires all of the consciousness, creativity, and potential you can muster in order to traverse, support, and come into harmony with your life, global changes, and the world.

Why You Might Want to Read It

This book is written primarily *to* people in business. Specifically, it is directed to those of you who see yourselves as leaders — whether in positions of power or not. Additionally, it is written *for* all of you who are leading us into our future and who view your work as sacred.

Successful but radical rethinking of leadership and business is required. It will only come as a result of being well equipped. As with any walk deep into the forest, it is wise to take whatever is necessary to make your way as safely as possible. Within the context of this book, "well equipped" means augmenting your conventional business skills, knowledge, and talent with deeper and fuller personal powers. You increase these powers through coming to know more about yourself, about how and what you think, about where you are learning and growing, and your depth of spirit.

You will find reading further of value if you:

- Want support for questioning your assumptions and beliefs.
- Have hopes of evoking change in the world, however large or small the change—and however large or small your world.
- Are exploring emerging paradigms of business leadership.
- Want vision and nourishment for bringing more of your authenticity and creativity forward in the workplace.
- Are interested in attaining more personal congruence and integrity through directly and openly merging work and spirit.
- Want to consider this path through the forest as an option for attending to leadership as sacred work.

A Brief "Field Guide" of Words

Language not only expresses reality, but forms it. The words you use and the definitions you give them reveal much about the world as you see it. Words define "reality."

Through global business and its widespread use of English, we are creating a global culture.

At the end of the twentieth century, English is the primary language of global organizations in general, and for the majority of global business organizations. As a result, English not only *expresses* the current business reality, but is *defining* it for the future across myriad economic, political, social, and ethnic boundaries. Thus, through global business and its widespread use of English, we are creating a global culture.

A step on the journey as a leader within business is developing deeper awareness of how you use language and the impact it has. Here is how I am defining some significant words in this book.

Assumption

An assumption is a supposition, the truth of which is taken for granted. "Assumption" and "belief" are used interchangeably.

Business

An archaic definition of business is "purposeful activity"—as is "busyness." "Business" denotes the world of corporations, for-profit organizations, the buying and selling of products and services, and financial transactions.

Challenging

"Challenging" has two very different meanings. One is "arousing competitive interest, thought, or action." Within business, this is a familiar definition. A second meaning is "stimulating or interesting," as in a stimulating or interesting problem or task. The definition you choose determines much about how you relate to challenges at work and in the world. The challenges themselves remain the same.

Evolution

Thomas Berry, a thinker and writer about life on earth, says that evolution has three fundamental dynamics:

- Increasing awareness or consciousness of the "self."
- Greater awareness of one another, or "intercommunion."
- Increasing differentiation and richer variety.

Global

Until recently, businesses referred to themselves almost exclusively as "international" or "multinational." The shift to "global," while subtle, is significant. Both international and multinational are based on nation-states and relationships between them. "Global," on the other hand, has nothing in particular to do with nations. Other meanings for the word are "universal" and "relating to a whole." Global goes far beyond geography. It contains a deeper, more essential notion of wholeness. Therefore, global business and global leaders, whether worldwide or not, simultaneously quest toward wholeness within themselves and for all life.

Journey

"Journey" comes from the French word *jour*, meaning "day"; it implies a day's work or a day's travel from one place to another. Thus, a journey crosses through both time and space, and implies arriving somewhere other than where you started.

Leadership

"Lead" comes from the Anglo-Saxon *laed*, "to set out on a quest, to navigate into the distant horizon." Leadership includes, but also extends far beyond, position power. In today's world, anyone who has the time, money, and energy to be reading this book is a potential global leader with the opportunity for doing sacred work. The vast majority of our fellow humans can see ahead only a few miles and a few meals—and even that requires good fortune.

Power

"Power" comes from the Old French word *poeir*, "to be able." Virtually all definitions in common usage relate to control, authority, or influence over others. In this book, "power" means a force coming from within. It is a *power to*: to harmonize with natural order, to let go, to pay attention, to find purpose and meaning, to think anew. What we already know has power over us, keeps us in chains, and keeps us from changing—especially if it seems "totally obvious." Our freedom and our future lie in the unknown, in the exploration of our "power to."

Practice

Playing the piano requires experience. Simply reading about the life of Chopin, or how baby grand pianos are made is insufficient. The *power* to play the piano *well* requires mastery which comes from sustained practice.

Responsibility

"Response" comes from the Latin *responsum*, "reply"; "ability" comes from the Latin *habilis*, for "apt or skillful." "Ability" also means "the quality or state of being able," as well as something for which one is responsible and trustworthy. Therefore, responsibility here means being able to respond skillfully and in a trustworthy manner to anything for which you are responsible.

Sacred

The Middle English word *sacren* meant "to consecrate, to devote, to make holy." The sacred is anything deserving reverence and respect. Historically, leadership in the secular world has not been considered sacred. In fact, in the West, sacred work has been viewed as that which is *other* than secular. Yet, everything you do is sacred, especially if you have the power to affect lives. What could be more sacred, more holy, than determining the nature of how we live? Life is the holiest of gifts.

Spirit and Spirituality

As with sacred, "spirit" and "spirituality" go beyond the domain of church or religion; they are life itself. Through spirit we infuse deeper meaning and purpose into our lives; we unleash our untapped, unlimited creative potential; we comprehend our connection to each other and all Life. "Spirit" comes from the Latin word *spiritus*, which means "to breathe in new life, to animate or enliven." Spirit is essential to life and goes with us wherever we go. We may choose *how* and *how much* we express our spirituality, but not *whether* we do it. Spirit informs work, and work is a primary venue for spiritual expression.

Work

Work means the labor, tasks, or duties you do in order to make your income; the effort you expend to overcome obstacles and achieve goals; and your means of making your contribution to the world.

World

"World" and "earth" have different meanings. "World" comes from the Old English word *woruld* for "human existence" and "the earthly state of human existence." "Earth," on the other hand, is the third planet from the sun. Therefore, we face the potential of the end of the world though not the end of the earth.

Barbara Shipka

Planet Earth
Vernal Equinox 1996

If you want the truth, you must write about yourself. I am the only truth I know.

—J. RHYS

PRELUDE

Directions in the Forest

Unless we change the direction we are headed in, we might end up where we are going.

—*Old Chinese proverb*

What Is Dying (or Transforming)?
What Is Being Born (or Wasted)?
Which Way to Go?

The Chinese *Tai Ji* symbol of yin and yang represents the ever-changing balance between complementarity and polarity. Each half of the symbol grows from a sliver to a bulb in relationship to the other; only together do they create a coherent whole. Each half helps the other maintain its shape and its integrity. Within each half lives a small dot of the opposite's primary nature. These dots not only represent the idea that each half contains some of its opposite; perhaps more significant, they represent the dynamic nature of the relationship between the two elements in that each half has the potential for *becoming* its opposite.

This simple and elegant symbol portrays much about life. It shows both unity and polarity; static form and the inevitability of change; separate identity and interconnectedness; and the presence within everything of its opposite. It is a symbol that

Tai Ji Symbol

transcends the dichotomy between "both/and" and "either/or," in that it contains both "both/and" *and* "either/or." Each half lives as itself, yet neither can live without the other. Each half grows and changes in its own right, yet neither evolves without the other.

"Part I: The Forest" has two seemingly opposite themes. Together they depict yin and yang. One theme names what is potentially dying and, because of this, our despair and loss. It portrays our global dilemmas, an urgency for changing our ways, and the possible demise of life on the earth. The other theme names what is being born and, because of it, our hope and joy. This second theme is about changing our thinking, creating a more viable world, and our potential for evolving to an all new way of being.

Two stories exemplify these themes. Each story represents a scenario of life in our times. While they appear opposite, each contains a measure of the other. Together they create a whole.

What Is Dying (or Transforming)?

One night in 1987 I had a dream:

A handsome, intelligent, well-dressed corporate businessman is driving as we wend our way. He goes slowly, using extreme caution to avoid the throngs of people moving in the opposite direction. They seem frightened as they coax children along and clutch meager belongings. "What's going on?" I ask. "It's because of the fire," he explains. "Oh, I see," I reply, though I have no idea what he is talking about. Not wanting to appear ignorant, I don't ask, "What fire?"

A six-foot-high concrete wall topped with jagged-edged glass from broken bottles—a common form of security in some parts of the world—surrounds the only tall building for miles around. (Enveloping the outer perimeter of the wall), a mass of humanity lives on the streets and in makeshift homes constructed of what others have discarded.

The building is beautiful! Passing through the gate, a sense of spaciousness, quiet, and ease embraces me. As we ascend to the top of the building, the seventh story, I say, "I'm struck by the urgent, frenetic mood outside the gate." "Yes," my colleague responds. "But, lucky for us, it's not something we have to worry about."

The seventh story is an elegant yet conservative reception space. Several others have already arrived. Most are men between thirty-five and fifty-five who appear to be highly successful executives like my colleague. There are only a few other women, and no children or old people. The mood is upbeat, jovial.

As I walk across the room, greeting people along the way, I glance out the windows to the south and see fire across the entire horizon. No trees or animals are in front of the fire—only dry savanna grass, and people on the move. A pit forms in my stomach as I notice my feelings of shock and terror.

I run from the room and down the stairs two at a time. I want to help; to offer my energy, my time, my intelligence. But what can I do? I run haphazardly through the streets and become just one more person among the teeming masses. I am dissipating my resources without having the slightest positive impact.

With a heavy heart, I retrace my steps. On my way back I glimpse creative attempts to survive the fire. One especially stands out: Two boys have rigged up a teeter-totter/pulley system over a sewer. Thus, one boy comes up to breathe as the other is lowered into the vat of sewage to cool off.

Passing through the gate, I re-enter the building. As I climb the stairs I encounter a young, dark-skinned woman descending. Her eyes downcast, she holds a newborn baby in her arms. Since she clearly doesn't live here, and since they are both soaked through, I imagine that someone gave her permission to use the shower. I think how this may be the last time they will be cool. For an instant I consider taking them upstairs with me. That, at least, would be something I could do.

As we meet, she looks directly and unabashedly into my eyes. I am stunned by the calm, the compassion, and the comprehension I see. I witness generations of ancient, timeless wisdom in her teenage face. Without a word she communicates that she knows I cannot take her and her child upstairs; that we all would be refused entrance. Tears fill my eyes as I receive her forgiveness and, at the same time, feel my despair and helplessness.

Entering the seventh story again I see beer and snacks being set out. People are conversing, laughing, and dancing. The fire is moving closer. The smoke finds its way to the windows. "Look!" I shout. "Please look! The fire is rapidly approaching. What are we going to do?" My colleague smiles consolingly and says, "Don't worry. It's okay. We'll all be okay as long as we stay up here." He pulls the curtains to block out the unpleasant sight. "It might get hot in here and become difficult to breathe. But we are survivors, after all. When the fire has passed we will go back downstairs and begin to rebuild." But I think to myself, "How can I ever leave this room again?"

What Is Being Born (or Wasted)?

Do you remember where you were, and what you were doing, when the first astronauts landed on the moon? If you are too young to remember the landing, you have an even more direct relationship with the changes occurring than those of us who watched the event live on television. It always has been your reality to "know" the whole earth. We have a poster of the earth hanging in our home. When my son, Michael, first began to speak and was asked where he was from, he said, "Earth"—and pointed to the poster. These days, at five years old, he still points to the poster and says, "I live on the brown area, right there." Never mind that he's pointing to Zimbabwe; he already has a mental construct of the whole earth. It's natural to him.

I have cable television for one primary reason: NASA TV. When a shuttle is on orbit, I leave the television tuned to channel 46B most of the time. That way, when the video cameras focus on the earth, I can witness our planet's magnificence and incredible beauty. I notice how thin the atmosphere is, and the blackness of space beyond.

In July of 1995, as I watched, U.S. astronauts and Russian cosmonauts linked up five hundred thousand pounds of machinery—the *Mir* space station and the shuttle *Atlantis*—while traveling at 17,500 miles per hour, 215 miles above the earth. The artfully completed first docking was off by two seconds and seven-tenths of an inch. The accomplishment was truly a testament to human creativity and ingenuity.

Rusty Schweickart, who flew on *Apollo 9*, speaks of seeing the earth from an orbit around the moon. The earth, he says,

> ... is so small and so fragile and such a precious little spot in that universe that you can block it out with your thumb and you realize on that small spot, that little blue and white thing, is everything that means anything to you—all of history and music and poetry and art and death and birth and love, tears, joy, games, all of it on that little spot that you can cover with your thumb. And you realize from that perspective that you've changed, that there's something new there, that the relationship is no longer what it was. (F. White, p.38)

We experience this change in our relationship with the earth without physically going to the moon. Look at Michael; look at the poster. The photo of the earth from space has become a common part of our daily lives. It appears on postcards and T-shirts, in advertising and as business logos. Yet, it still moves something very deep within us. As Peter Russell wrote in *The Global Brain*, "... in spite of all this exposure, the picture still strikes a very deep chord, and none of its magnificence has been lost."

Which Way to Go?

Global, organizational, and individual challenges are powerfully and richly mirrored by the seventh-story dream. The challenges we face are many and great. The most significant challenge of all, however, reiterated in many ways throughout the book, is identifying how we *think* (or don't think) that is harming us. For example, a cultural assumption that for centuries has fueled Western thinking is that we are separate from the rest of life, and that the rest of life is here to serve us—in other words, that the rest of the earth is for us to control and use in any way we "need." We have believed that we can understand life by breaking it into component parts. (Remember dissecting that frog in high-school biology?) We also have believed that we are material and static "things," more than unfolding, evolving processes. In fact, you are not the person you used to be; within seven years, every cell in your body is renewed. I say "we have believed" because we are coming to discover that the world may differ from our common beliefs and assumptions.

We are coming to discover that the world may differ from our common beliefs and assumptions.

What you believe affects how you make business decisions. Those business decisions contribute to the making or unmaking of our future. In the dream I recounted, do you believe the fire is a fire that destroys, or fire that transforms—a fire of death, or a fire resulting in new life? Can the destructive force of fire be challenged or redirected into elements of service—into heat, energy, protection, mesmerizing beauty, for example?

Being one who is on the seventh story, what do you believe about your ability to survive the effects of the fire by staying where you are and by drawing the drapes? Your assumptions—about yourself, about global change, and about business being part of, or somehow exempt from, the larger whole—are determining the future now.

What if challenging our cultural beliefs and assumptions built up over centuries brings with it the risk of being excluded from the seventh story? Yet, the dream suggests that leadership means attending to more than what is on the seventh story; that if you want a world in which to do business and thrive, you must lead in ways that address global challenges.

You, as a business leader in the industrialized world, hold much of the resources, power, and energy to resist or support what wants to die, and what hopes to be born. You have an important, indeed crucial, role to play. In order to choose well, you must come as fully as possible into the fullness and wholeness of your creative potential and your personal power.

As we change what we think, we change all human-made systems.

As I think about our potential directions and resulting possible futures, I notice some basic assumptions I hold that undergird my written words:

- *We are life and part of the natural order of the universe.* We are of the same material as stars and lilies. We grow and change individually and collectively. We evolve. We experience beauty and bliss, health and happiness, by coming into harmony with the patterns of the universe. We suffer from the illusion that we can control the natural patterns.
- *We have the ability to notice what we think.* We also have the ability to make conscious choices about what we do with what we think. Every organization and institution we have is a result of what we have thought, and it continues to exist because of what we continue to think. Organizations and institutions are agreements we make and keep. When we change our thinking and, thus our agreements, our institutions change as well. Therefore, as we change what we think, we change all human-made systems.
- *We have the possibility to directly engage in our own evolution.* We do so through our consciousness and our creativity. Doing this takes deliberate attention and discipline.

THE FOREST I

Demanding Challenges

Life is paradox and contradiction. Whether your current tendency leans toward despair and denial about our global dilemmas, or instead toward hope and awareness, doesn't really matter. Both are true. Both help us see our work. They inform each other.

The first three chapters define the forest—the context for change—through focusing on our dilemmas, the urgency of our needs, and the possible extinction of life. In order, these three chapters briefly explore the nature and scope of:

Our Global Emergency
Related Business Issues
Individual Leadership Challenges

Chapter 1

Global Emergency

Anyone who recognizes what is going on in the world and is not insecure is just not awake.

A *FORTUNE 500* CEO,
SPEAKING AT A *FORTUNE* MAGAZINE CEO CONFERENCE

Systems That Are Not Life-Serving
Interlocking Crises
Economic and Social Imbalance

Applying more pressure to what we don't like tends to create more of what we don't want—witness the "war on poverty," the "war on drugs," or the "war on crime." We continue to lose these "wars." Instead, we have more homeless and disenfranchised people; narcotics organizations developing dangerous new drugs and new means of smuggling them; and overcrowded prisons. In their book *The Soul of Economics*, Breton and Largent (1991) write that the two largest "industries" in the world today are illegal drugs and weapons.

The global issues and dilemmas facing us are of unknown magnitude. Simply *comprehending* their depth and breadth is an enormous challenge. If we use history as our guide, we can look back upon times of massive change—and see massive attendant human suffering.

Systems That Are Not Life-Serving

Daniel Quinn's novel *Ishmael* is the tale of a relationship between a teacher and student. The teacher describes how most of human civilization, who he calls "the Takers," lives in defiance of natural law. To illustrate our discord with natural life processes, he asks his student to imagine someone leaping off a high cliff in a pedal-driven, wing-flapping "flying machine." The "flyer" pedals away and flaps his wings with the wind in his hair. At first, all is well. He feels euphoric at the freedom of "flight." Except he isn't really flying—he's in free fall. When finally he notices the ground rushing up to meet him, his thought is: "Well, so far so good. I've been flying very successfully. I'll pedal faster, flap my wings harder."

The teacher makes the connection to civilization's "flight" from the laws that govern the rest of the biological community. With our freedom of flight has come the alluring wonders of urbanization, science and technology, and literacy. Some people in flight look down, and what they see alarms them; to them, it looks as though the ground is rushing up. Others merely shrug and say, "We've come all this enormous way, and haven't even been so much as scratched. It's true the ground seems to be rising up to meet us, but that just means we'll have to pedal a little harder." But, oddly enough, the harder and more efficiently they pedal, the worse conditions become.

We must take seriously that what we do, or fail to do matters enormously.

You and I are the ones pedaling as we are free-falling perilously toward the ground. We have our work cut out for us. Many may say to us, "It's worked until now," or "So far so good," or "If it ain't broke, don't fix it," or "Someone will figure something out." We must not believe these voices; what is more, we must challenge them. We must take seriously that what we do, or fail to do, matters enormously. We must prepare ourselves and our organizations to lead in a truly challenging world with systems out of balance and life in free fall.

When working with systems in change we look for points of highest leverage, points where one "small" change, if made well, affects everything. Change made *well* is the key, because change has potential for engendering more harm than good. Think of the last forty years of international economic development, for example. With the perspective of time, it seems that much of what we have done in the world comes up wanting. A difficult question is increasingly raised: Who has "economic development" around the world really served? In many cases governments are unable to pay their debts; people want what is out of their reach; and the local cultural fabric is painfully rent, with families split apart by the promise of the city's bright lights and subsistence farms turned over to cash crops.

We covered a fifty-mile stretch of road, round trip, from the capital, Mogadishu, to refugee camps in the south of Somalia about once a week. The road had once been a dirt track; then, in the interest of development, it was paved. On our first trip south, we noticed several drivers, obviously familiar with the route, leaving the paved road periodically and driving in the ditch for mile after mile. Hussein, who was driving, stayed on the pavement for a while, but soon found driving almost impossible because of potholes too big to drive around or too deep to drive through. Besides, the vehicles in the ditch were making much better time than we were. We joined them. Given the sandy desert foundation under the pavement and the lack of resources for maintenance, what had been intended for improvement had instead become an obstacle. The drivers had built themselves a "new" road: a dirt track just like the original one, except that it was twenty-five feet farther east for driving north, and twenty-five feet farther west for driving south.

Behind my house in Mogadishu was a water tower. Young boys with donkey carts lined up day after day to fill their oil drums with water. They supplied the entire section of the city around me. One night I awoke to an enormous crashing. The water tower had fallen over; it had been built on sand. For several days the boys had no access to water. My section of the city had no access to water. Eventually the well was made usable again by lowering a bucket with a rope attached. The water tower was never rebuilt but the boys' water businesses boomed again.

Interlocking Crises

David Korten, in *Getting to the 21st Century: Voluntary Action and the Global Agenda*, writes about three interlocking aspects of what he calls "the crisis we face": dehumanizing poverty, environmental degradation, and communal violence. Korten states that when you have any one of the three, the other two follow. Thus, communal violence begets poverty and a degraded environment; dehumanizing poverty results in a degraded environment and violence; and a degraded environment leads to poverty and violence. He says these three "pose a threat to human civilization," and that "[u]nless adequate corrective action is forthcoming, the North may find that the current Southern experience is a window into its own future—not the reverse." (p.1)

Thus, we must redefine what it means to live together *viably*. To take but one example: During the 1990s, our population is growing by 250,000 people every day. We are adding approximately one billion new people to the planet between 1990 and 2000, with 900,000,000 of them being in the less economically developed parts of the world. By 2006 we will add yet another billion. Aside from such evident direct implications as crowding and increased poverty, many other implications surface: more fossil fuels spewed into an atmosphere only twelve miles high, with whole national economies dependent on them; two billion more people, age sixteen and under, headed into the "job market." Where will that fuel come from? Where will the resulting pollution go? Where will those two billion jobs come from? The entire system is interconnected. Denying global warming and imagining creating enough new jobs both come from conventional thinking insufficient to treat even the symptoms, let alone the causes, of global dilemmas in our interdependent world. As Rita Mae Brown said, "Insanity is doing the same thing over and over and expecting different results."

Economic and Social Imbalance

In his February 1994 *Atlantic Monthly* article "The Coming Anarchy," Robert D. Kaplan writes, in the words of the article's subtitle, about "How scarcity, crime, overpopulation, tribalism, and disease are rapidly destroying the social fabric of our planet." He paints a stark and revealing picture of both the present and our near-term future by illustrating the trends he identifies as shaping the disorder ahead. For example, he writes of West Africa as "becoming *the* symbol of worldwide demographic, environmental, and societal stress, in which criminal anarchy emerges as the real 'strategic' danger. Disease, overpopulation, unprovoked crime, scarcity of resources, refugee migrations, the increasing erosion of nation-states and international borders, and the empowerment of private armies, security firms, and international drug cartels are now most tellingly demonstrated through a West African prism."

Globally, we are experiencing social and infrastructural disintegration. The relationship between government and commerce provides a primary example of a world out of balance. Government and commerce, as we know them in the West, were set up to balance each other. As we see our economic system become global—while we maintain, at best, a nation-state governance system—that balance is most likely gone forever. In fact, as nation-states break into ethnic units in many parts of the world, the scales are becoming even more uneven. What will be the new balance?

Systems that do not serve life, but rather produce interlocking crises resulting from imbalances, are examples of where our current thinking is leading us—and make clear the scale of the challenges we face. We believe we are separate from nature, that we can be successful over the long term by treating symptoms, and that we can effectively act without understanding the interdependent implications of our actions. For us to create a viable world, all of these assumptions about systems and what constitutes a "whole" must change quickly—and within a large number of people.

Chapter 2

Related Business Issues and Dilemmas

Business has become, in this last half century, the most powerful institution on the planet. The dominant institution in any society needs to take responsibility for the whole...

—WILLIS HARMAN

Survival

Global Systems and Individual People

Assumptions About What Business Is and Can Do

Those on the seventh story in the dream represent only a minute segment of the global population in real life; they are the business leaders of the industrialized world. Dreams are revealing because they show depth of belief, if not necessarily truth. My daytime experience with business leaders, especially one-on-one, is that they do care about the rest of the world. They feel deeply about the communities where they live and work, about ethical behaviors and policies, and about their children's future.

Yet, while they may not be partying, many shut the windows and pull the drapes against the sight of the flames and the smell of the smoke in the larger world. Many believe they are *required* to block out the fire and the people it will touch in order to remain successful; others believe that all they must do is comply with what is required politically and socially.

Survival

Survival depends on our ability to gracefully transform our thinking in harmony with the world's transformation. Looked at in one way, the fire in the dream can represent transformational change across the entire horizon.

Transformation is a specific and unique form of change. A lake freezes in winter. Water is changed to ice, yes; but the change is temporary. Under the right conditions, the ice may be returned to virtually the same water. Fire is different. Wood becomes heat, ash, and smoke. The heat, ash, and smoke, however, will never again be the same trees. The transformed molecules of the wood contribute to the nourishment of new trees, but they will never return to the wood they were.

Transformation is radical change. We move into totally new, undefined territory during times of transformation. The outcome is unknown, and often unpredictable. This implies being "out of control" in conventional terms.

In a transforming world, a burning world, major challenges face businesses and those of you who lead them. You must guide your business through the transformation. You must lead your organization even when you and others feel afraid. And you must overcome your fear, because fear causes you and your organization to become rigid and fragile. It diminishes your ability to be creative, generous, open, vital, resilient.

Global businesses are a primary holder of resources, and they comprise a stage for enormous untapped creativity.

It is critical that businesses survive and succeed. Although you and I may not always like what they do or represent, global businesses form the infrastructure that is working in today's world. They are a primary holder of resources and they comprise a stage for enormous untapped creativity.

Global Systems and Individual People

At the same time that we work to keep businesses alive, we must transform them from "machines that chew people up and spit them out"—as one client once said to me—into humane instruments of service, with initiative and the ability to respond to needs ranging from the most global to the most personal. We need businesses able to respond at a global level because we want a planet on which to do business. We need businesses able to respond at a personal level because, for many in the West, the workplace is one of the most important places in our lives. It is through our work that many of us seek to be of service in meaningful and purposeful ways.

At the global level, we confront all of the challenges noted in the previous chapter—and more besides. There is pressure to compete on the global stage; to build partnerships and alliances with other businesses while maintaining a unique niche; to be lean and then even leaner, to move fast and then even faster.

At the personal or individual level, the contract between businesses and employees is changing dramatically. Historically based on reciprocal exchange, that contract works only as long as employees *and* organizations feel that they are receiving in balance with what they are giving. The essential nature of the contract remains, but the terms of reciprocity—and the value we place on the contract itself—are changing. For example, most employees understand that loyalty and job security until retirement are artifacts of another time. For their part, businesses understand that they cannot expect employees to "put up or shut up." As a consequence, employees can expect more responsibility—and, in return, express more creativity—during their employment. And businesses can expect to distribute more power and leadership—and, in return, to count on employees helping make their businesses more effective and productive.

The path to achieving such dramatic change can be painful. It upsets long-held expectations; some people get caught in the middle. In a recent leadership development program, a number of us were talking about "shared leadership." A manufacturing first-line supervisor said, "I'm here because my boss said I had to come. What I want to know is, when is it my turn to be in charge? When I came to work for this company twenty-five years ago, if I complained I was told, 'Look! You don't like the way things are? There's the door.' Now I'm being told I have to listen and be more responsive to the people who report to me. If I don't learn to be a more participative supervisor, I'm told, 'Look! You don't like the way things are? There's the door.' Again, I want to know: When do I get to make that comment to someone else?"

Though they may not get to be "in charge," people are indeed being asked to take more responsibility, to learn how to think strategically as well as tactically, to solve problems and make decisions on their own or in teams, to single-handedly complete tasks that used to be done by two or three people—and to figure out how to improve processes and efficiency enough to accomplish their "megajobs" without completely burning out. More and more employee tasks and responsibilities are crossing over into the domain traditionally reserved for managers.

In reciprocity for businesses' increased expectations of employees, the employees, as individuals and as a collective also have a changing sense of the conditions of a fair exchange. Many desire benefits that include, but go far beyond, the traditional rewards of a paycheck, medical insurance, and vacation. They desire—and, in many cases, also expect—meaning, growth, learning, and support. They expect respect, an opportunity to express themselves creatively, and the chance to achieve more of their potential.

As in those popular three-dimensional computer images that suddenly seem to leap from one-dimensional to multidimensional depending on the focus of your eyes, a figure-ground shift in our perception of business is also possible. Such a shift in perception changes everything. An example would be for businesses and business leaders to perceive themselves as servants to both individuals and the larger global system, rather than as the victim or the controller of either. Business is positioned to be a conductor, a conduit, and a catalyst between the people with their imaginations on the one hand, and the world with its needs on the other. Business has an enormous opportunity to serve as a primary bridge between human creativity and the potential for whole systems change and transformation.

Assumptions About What Business Is and Can Do

Seeing the world in this way points toward some areas inviting deeper investigation: What is required for businesses to be successful? Who does business serve? To what end? One collective belief is that profitability is measured monetarily, and that "doing good" is primarily in the domain of community-relations departments. Said another way, the belief is that profitability and serving the larger good are more or less mutually exclusive objectives.

One small example of current business thinking is illustrated through prevailing views of "expert" consulting. I recently listened to a colleague describe her difficulty finding a resource she needed. Usually, I am more likely to see what is missing than present in myself; but this time I saw myself as having all of the attributes she needed. When I pointed this out to her, some tacit, unnamed attributes came forth. "You know how it is," she said; "you can't be an expert in your own backyard. You've got to be from more than fifty miles away, and have a 'name.'" In terms of our current paradigm, she's thinking clearly. She's accurately considering what is credible to managers in the corporation that employs her. Yet such thinking unconsciously perpetuates old patterns, in at least two ways: It is expensive and unnecessarily consumptive to fly people all over; and it creates hardship conditions for family units. I have several consulting colleagues who live in the San Francisco Bay area; many must fly to work.

We must find ways to bring profitability and self-interest together with compassion and responsibility for the well-being of our whole system. The role that business can play in the world today is colossal. You who are in leadership determine, through the choices and decisions you make daily, whether or not you and your business serve all life and evolution.

Chapter 3

Crisis and Opportunity for Leaders

I am only one; but I am still one. I cannot do everything, but still I can do something. I will not refuse to do the something I can do.

—HELEN KELLER

Breaking Our Cultural Trance
Finding the Depth of Our Creativity
Questioning Personal Beliefs
Fully Living Our Daily Lives

When you think about our growing population, decaying infrastructures, disappearing forests and wildlife, increasing violence, and failing social institutions, how do you feel? Do you ever feel scared? Do you ever feel helpless, out of control, overwhelmed? Do you ever find that you practically stop breathing? These are natural feeling responses, given what is going on right now on the earth.

Breaking Our Cultural Trance

Sometimes we wish for someone to sing us lullabies, someone to assure us that everything is not so bad. But even lullabies don't always have peaceful endings: in "Rock-a-bye Baby," both the baby and its cradle come tumbling down when the bough breaks. We live in a forest where both humanity and its cradle are overwhelming the bough of the tree that holds us.

An attitude we carry, in a phrase, is "We're so successful and you can't argue with success": but human behavior is on a trajectory leading to its own destruction. Can we really expect that "someone" is going to figure a way out of the dilemmas we currently face? Even more specifically, can you and I, providing leadership in business—the most powerful infrastructure of our day—really believe that "someone" other than ourselves is determining our present and future? Who else might it be?

At some level you know there is truth in what I am saying. If you don't (or think you don't), ask the children in your life—then, listen to them. Many children see adult denial very clearly. Others, unwilling or unable to speak about it, act *out* what we are unwilling to act *on*. Others despair at the future being left to them. Our children fear the depth of what they *know* to be true without volumes of "proof," for they have not yet learned the myth that humans are exempt from working within natural laws.

Finding the Depth of Our Creativity

People in corporate organizations are called "human resources" —a dehumanizing term that regards us as commodities, like electricity, trees, or money, to be used for the benefit of the business. In fact, commodities can be used up. We are not "human resources" or "headcount" or "manpower." We are human beings with leadership skills, whether working as a CEO or as an assembler in a factory, who are in relationship with one another. We must reframe our experiences and our value in organizations, and come to better understand that we are not commodities but communities.

> *We must reframe our experiences and our value in organizations, and come to better understand that we are not commodities but communities.*

Individually, each of us has *access* to unlimited capacity within ourselves. As a human community, we bring together myriad resources representing a limitless spectrum of possibility. But under the current structures and strictures of business organizations, most of us do not believe we *should* bring all of what we know or can do to our working environments. At present there are rules and taboos about what we can legitimately bring into our workplaces. The result is that many of us believe we are supposed to check our deepest personal selves—our inner lives, our soul's development—at the door of our workplaces. This assumption prevents us from bringing some of the most powerful and creative parts of ourselves to our jobs.

Beyond that, if we hide the deepest parts of ourselves that are *known* to us, what about those parts that we haven't yet consciously tapped—resources that are waiting to be accessed? We have no idea how brilliant and creative we can be. As far as we know, human creativity and ingenuity are unlimited.

Questioning Personal Beliefs

Questioning your personal beliefs fundamentally underlies everything else. You must identify and question *what* you believe—about what is appropriate to bring into your workplace, about what adds value (even about what "value" is), and about *why* you believe what you do. Then, you must have the courage to be the change you want to see, and to encourage and honor the change you see others being.

In questioning my own thinking, I contemplated why beginning to write this book was an enormous challenge for me. What was my resistance about? Three limiting beliefs surfaced.

First, how can I be so audacious? How can *I* write about walking a path toward a deeper capacity for leading? I am humbled. I have an opportunity and a responsibility to witness my beliefs and my denial, and to take careful note of where I am in my development, as I write about as well as practice what I suggest we *become*. One growth task for me is to experience humility without allowing it to silence me. I also have to learn how to forgive myself for whatever part of my "humility" might be low self-esteem, whether of the self-effacing or arrogant variety. Unlike Gandhi in the following story, I am still eating the "sugar" of almost everything I write about.

One day a mother brought her son to see Gandhi. She said to him, "My son admires you and will take to heart anything you tell him. Would you please advise him to stop eating sugar? It is harming his health." Gandhi asked the woman to return with her son in a month. Puzzled, the mother left with her son. One month later they returned. Gandhi advised the boy to stop eating sugar. The mother then asked, "Why did you ask us to wait a month? Why didn't you say those simple words to him a month ago?" Gandhi replied, "Because at that time I was eating sugar myself.

How could I sincerely recommend that your son stop when I hadn't?"

Secondly, I have feared that the written word will lock my soul in time and space. In many cultures people do not allow their photographs to be taken, because they fear the images will steal away their souls. The process of writing sometimes feels that deep, that threatening, for me as well. I will, no doubt, change my mind, enlarge my field of view, or deepen my thoughts after the book is released. But what matters is the essence behind what I am writing. It attracts like-minded and like-hearted others and, thus, my experience ultimately becomes one of liberation and connection rather than capture.

A third belief is related to the investment required to write a book. It means hours and hours alone, rewrite after rewrite. For what payback? Consulting has served me well and long. It is difficult to shift my focus for a time. This shift of focus is a personal choice; but it is also something much larger. Have you ever been compelled in a direction against "rational" evidence? So it is for me. Behind all of my limiting beliefs is my fear of not being "rational."

My image is of an enormous steam locomotive chugging forward with power and force. I hold a rope tied to the back of the engine. Digging my heels into the earth, I try to stop it from moving forward. It gains speed and momentum with each passing second. Yes, I have choice. I can resist and get bloody heels—and eventually fall forward onto my face; I can let go of the rope and be left without the power of the locomotive. Or I can get on, enjoy the ride, and see the locomotive as a resource.

For now, writing is the locomotive. Trying to hold the locomotive back comes from fearing I may not earn enough money to support myself and my son while I'm on this ride. And I wonder: Can I, will I, say something of value that others are hungry for? Yet perhaps maybe most fearsome of all is another consideration: What if the results are truly grand? What if the locomotive decides to leave the tracks and fly? What if I am truly humbled? Then what will I do?

As Marianne Williamson wrote in *A Return to Love*:

Our deepest fear is not that we are inadequate. Our deepest fear is that we are powerful beyond measure. It is our light, not our darkness, that most frightens us. We ask ourselves, "Who am I to be brilliant, gorgeous, talented and fabulous?" Actually, who are you not to be? You are a child of God. Your playing small doesn't serve the world. There's nothing enlightened about shrinking so that other people won't feel insecure around you... We were born to make manifest the glory of God that is within us; it's not just in some of us; it's in everyone. And as we let our own light shine, we unconsciously give other people permission to do the same. As we are liberated from our own fear, our presence automatically liberates others. (p. 165)

Fully Living Our Daily Lives

You and your organization are being challenged to attend to global systems and re-establish global balance. You must keep your business successful through tumultuous times of transformation while also turning it into a bridge between global need and individual potential. You must redefine and redesign the paths through which individual contributions are made, and find ways to help draw out the untapped creativity within everyone around you while building a community that is of service.

As if that isn't enough, you must live your daily life, do your work, love and care for your family and other loved ones, pay your bills, have fun, maintain health and balance... You face a daunting task, indeed! You must find the particulars of balance along this path, which hugs the edge of a cliff. "Part II: The Path," which offers one possible path among many, consists of eight powers for achieving more balance and for leading well during these complex and profound times, is intended to support you in your walk.

THE FOREST II

Envisioning Possibilities

Now, with the challenges squarely in front of us, we move to hope, vision, and change. The experience of space flight, whether direct or indirect, has affected our perceptions of reality and our place in it. Living in the time of seeing the earth as a whole against an "empty" black backdrop has changed what it means to be a human being, much like the shift from nomadic life to living around a well changed what it meant to be a human being thousands of years ago.

Seeing the forest as full of hope comes from focusing on our ability to change our thinking, our creativity and potential, and our opportunity to serve during this evolution to an all new way of being.

It's All in Our Minds
Seeing the Garden in a Whole New Way
Bridge People

Chapter 4

It's All in Our Minds

No problem can be solved from the same consciousness that created it. We must learn to see the world anew.

—ALBERT EINSTEIN

Thinking Beyond Convention
We Create Our Future
Assumptions and Reality

Thinking Beyond Convention

In *New World New Mind*, Robert Ornstein and Paul Ehrlich write, "The human mental system is failing to comprehend the modern world." They suggest that the evolution of our minds has not kept pace with what we have created, and vividly illustrate their point by noting that we have not evolved beyond seeing danger as a bear at the door of the cave. We respond or react to what is most immediate. Public interest can be sparked by the plight of two whales drowning in the Arctic Ocean, but is far more difficult to maintain for the plight of life in the oceans in general.

The evolution of our minds has not kept pace with what we have created.

We get stuck because we believe we can change and remake our world in conventional ways. To follow Ornstein and Erlich's example, conventional "solutions" to seeing a bear at the door of the cave would be to hide far back in the cave, build a fire, throw sticks and stones, or scream to scare the bear away. We might even try to kill the bear with a spear. But, except for *that* moment with *that* bear, nothing has fundamentally changed. Even after the bear is gone we still live in the cave, and other bears are still in the forest.

We Create Our Future

If conventional solutions had been the basis for the creative inventions and innovations of the space program, no one would have circled weightlessly around the earth—let alone the moon. To create a more viable future, we must understand that we create our future day by day. In order to create our future in ways that serve us, we must evaluate everything differently.

The disparaging phrase "It's all in your *mind*" is often used in everyday language to imply "You don't know what you're talking about," or "What you're experiencing isn't what's really happening." Let's change the emphasis to "It's *all* in your mind." How we create our reality is a complex, metaphysical subject, and I'm not an expert at describing it; so let's stay practical. The definitions we use determine our assumptions, and the assumptions we carry determine our definitions.

Our world might be very different if the majority of us defined success differently.

Let's take "success" as an example. Within our society the dominant view of success is based on how much money one has, the volume of "output" one generates, or how much power one has over others. Our world might be very different if the majority of us defined success differently. For example, the most successful people might be those who walked as lightly upon the earth as possible and consumed the least materially, while still managing to find engaging and unique ways to live in wonderful comfort. Success might mean knowing that everything we need will be available when we need it; that we needn't accumulate and acquire out of fear of not having enough.

Redefining success might mean that the most successful business leaders would be those who put service over self-interest; those who encourage and reward true innovation in marketplace choices, instead of simply adding another to the fifty variations on the same theme already available; and those who focus intently and deeply on supporting themselves and everyone they touch in becoming more and more human. Successful leaders would be those who consciously *avoid* accumulating power *over* others and consuming natural resources. Success in leadership would result from skillfully generating power *with* others and evoking the sacred work of leadership from every person in the organization.

The bottom line of successful businesses would still be monetary profit—but only in the context of leaving the physical earth, and all life the business touches, not only as good but *better* than it was before. A core responsibility of business would be to generate means and milieu for as many humans as possible to make contributions toward creating a better world. A successful business would be one that knew not only when to stop growing *quantitatively*, but also how to continue to grow *qualitatively*. A primary measure of a successful business would be that it wasted nothing and created products that lasted a lifetime or more and wasted nothing in the process.

You may think such possibilities for redefining success are too far out on the edge; or you may think they are obvious. Both are true. There are people within our culture who define success in these ways already. All of this is possible. It just isn't easy to achieve within our current agreements and assumptions.

Assumptions and Reality

"Assumptions" and "reality" are frequently entirely different. There are some givens for life on earth that we can agree on as being real—such as we need air to breathe. Beyond similar fundamentals, much more of what we agree upon and *call* reality is at least relative, if not accurate. For example, even though we know the earth is rotating, we say that the sun rises in the morning and sets in the evening. While such an inaccuracy is benign, many inaccurate assumptions and agreements that we act on are far more dangerous. In the West, for hundreds of years we have assumed ourselves machines with component parts in a machine universe. That assumption leads to the next: that we can be separate from nature. Other assumptions then get built on those two and affect everything about what it means to be alive and human.

Thus, in great measure, "reality" is ALL in our minds. We become so certain that our assumptions are truth that we call them reality and, in time many become reality. In other words, underlying assumptions we agree upon result in our beliefs, attitudes and behaviors; our beliefs, attitudes and behaviors determine our essential agreements about life, the way the world works, what's possible, and what is right and what is wrong. Out of those assumptions come our agreements about what is business, what defines success, what work is, how we relate to each other, and all of our other specifics.

Beliefs become so ingrained as "truth" that we see them as the only way things can be, as self-evident, as reality. A sweet example occurs in the Spielberg fantasy film, "ET." As the children help the endearing alien return home, Elliot, ET's closest earth friend, says to one of the older boys, "He's a man from outer space and we're taking him to his spaceship." The older boy asks, "Well, can't he just beam up?" Elliot, in an exasperated tone responds, "This is REALITY, Greg!"

Fundamental underlying assumptions run deep and are pervasive. Even being able to see beyond some of our assumptions does not make it easy to change your behaviors. When I built my home I wanted to make it ecologically sound by placing it appropriately on the land, using toxic free materials, making it energy efficient, and supporting environmentally conscious businesses — all the while having it be a work of art. "Supply and demand," however, does not currently easily support me, as a middle-class person, in realizing my dream. I encountered problems that left me feeling disappointed and less than successful in achieving my goal. Many choices I wished to make would have raised the cost of the building beyond my budget. The quality of product of some environmentally sensitive companies was less than I wanted. The mortgage company would only finance if I used conventional materials. Very little within the community at large, other than my architect, supported me in making ecologically viable choices. I did what I could. Nonetheless, even with my awareness, I have contributed to majority assumptions by constructing one more ecologically compromised building.

Systemic change of independent individual and cultural assumptions comes as a result of one, then two, then more individuals changing their minds through exploring their deeply held assumptions and testing these sometimes newly named assumptions against "reality." Eventually, when a critical mass of people have explored and tested for themselves—often through deep conversation, dialogue, and inquiry—change for the whole society is possible. We can and do change our minds. Thus, over time, the definition of "reality" also changes. That "reality" is what we think it is today is one of the first assumptions we need to explore and test. Things are not as they seem.

With ability and willingness to go deeply to the roots of our thinking, we have the possibility of creating anew, of attending to cause rather than symptom, of claiming a most unique and precious gift: our power to discern what we think and to reframe and alter it if we wish. Such opportunity for positive change is collectively *in* our power. Collectively, it *is* our power.

Chapter 5

Seeing the Garden in a Whole New Way

*At first people refuse to believe that a strange
new thing can be done, then they begin to hope it
can't be done. They hope it can't be done because
it means seeing the garden in a whole new way.
Then they see it can be done. Then it is done and
all the world wonders why it was not done
centuries before.*

—FRANCES HODGSON BURNETT
The Secret Garden

A Focus
Individual and Systems Change
Visions
Organizations Are Agreements

A Focus

The most daunting task we must accomplish is seeing the garden in a whole new way. And it is required. In fact, it is *all* that is required. Seeing the garden in a whole new way may sound simple, but it is profoundly complex. It is where challenges and potential meet.

The good news is that the new seeing has already begun. We have seen the oneness of all humanity, indeed all life, through the astronauts' direct experience and through photographs of the earth from space. As we glimpse the garden in a whole new way, the "strange new things to be done" will become clearer and clearer to those who must lead us into this new perspective. What Frances Hodgson Burnett wrote for children is even more true for adults: once we step into this new perspective, "Then they see it can be done." With passing time the things to be done will seem less and less strange.

But it's *work*—sometimes unfamiliar work. Perhaps we can't find the hoe and have to make do with some other tool. The deer and rabbits are enjoying the newly sprouting plants and we wonder which to support: the animals, the plants, ourselves, or all three. The rains haven't come, so we must water the garden day after day. Many of us may not see the fruits of our extra labor; it will be our children who reap what we sow. It is tempting to be overwhelmed by the magnitude of our task.

Individual and Systems Change

Twenty-five years ago, I smoked. I smoked in university class-rooms; on airplanes, the minute the sign went off; in restaurants, before, between, and after courses; in cars driving through long, cold, enclosed Minnesota winters. I don't remember noticing how it affected those around me, or that others found it rude of me to light up. Nor do I remember asking permission.

In the seventies, changes began to occur—changes that offer a concrete example of simultaneous, interdependent change in my mind and in my community. Minnesota was the first state to enact a law requiring restaurants to provide a non-smoking section. With that, a new question was regularly asked of me, one that forced me to notice and choose: "Smoking or non-smoking?" Only a few years later, Northwest Airlines used their non-smoking policy as an advertising advantage. On their ticket jackets and in their airline magazine a map of North America was drawn with the continental United States highlighted; written across it was the phrase, "Our Non-Smoking Section." Though many smokers were outraged, Northwest's decision to take this step in the face of potential hostility was crucial both to affecting the change and to leading us to realize that the majority point of view was changing.

By that time, I had changed my mind too. I—who was certain I could not quit smoking, certain that I would take my last puff on my deathbed—had quit smoking! How did that happen? The changing laws and policies had an effect; but things were changing at other levels as well. One by one, many of my friends quit smoking. More messages about developing a healthy lifestyle began to appear. They had greater impact on me than the ones about how I was going to die from smoking. A developing collective awareness supported me in making change. Of course, I still had to quit.

Now I can go for months without being in the presence of cig-arette, cigar, or pipe smoke. None of the businesses for whom I consult allow smoking on their premises. In one, on below-zero winter days, people must hike to their cars—which often are parked blocks away for smoke breaks.

This dramatic change, occurring over a brief period of time, offers us a template of the interactive nature of individual and systems change. Some people still smoke, of course, and tobacco companies are expanding into new markets globally. Nonetheless, if change can happen in one place, in one time, it demonstrates potential for change in other places and times. Seeing the garden anew, doing the "strange new things" we once refused to believe could be done, is a *developmental, iterative process.*

Visions

While "viability" holds more hope and wholeness than "sustain-ability," sustainability is still the common word used to describe a workable future. Willis Harman names several conditions we must meet in order to best ensure the sustainability of human society on earth, including:

- That the planetary life-support systems—air, water, plant and animal life—must work together in support of each other.
- That we seek fairness for all people as a means of developing greater global stability.
- That everyone be given an opportunity to contribute and to be appreciated in return.
- That we support a diversity of cultures, so that we have resilience.
- That we rethink what national and global "security" means.

Harman's conditions closely parallel Thomas Berry's conditions for the evolution of life mentioned in the "Field Guide" of the Preface.

As we weave our way through Bangkok traffic beyond my imagining, my friend Char explains, "This is what it's like living here. I always take a book with me when I go by taxi because traffic can turn a twenty-minute commute into a three-hour ordeal."

"And look at those fifteen-story buildings, Barbara," her husband, Terry, exclaims. "They are a disaster waiting to happen because local fire equipment can only reach the fifth floor."

Once we reach the central city, we only walk a couple of blocks before my lungs ache and I have difficulty breathing. Even though it's the middle of the day, the sun is red. The air is the worst I've ever experienced, indoors or out. Bangkok may be a harbinger of the future urban experience in cities around the globe.

This illustration demonstrates the danger of transgressing merely one of Harman's conditions: the necessity of all planetary life-support systems supporting each other. We cannot tell from the story itself whether the others are upheld or not; but it shows grimly that violating even one of the conditions creates what is evidently an unsustainable scenario.

It doesn't have to be that way. Two weeks later I share a meal with my friends Tami and Api, with Api's family in Indonesia. Api says, "Recently the village council, the elders, seriously considered buying a tractor. My father is relating their deliberations to me." His father spoke in Indonesian, and Api translated for me. "'On the one hand,' one elder said, 'a tractor would be much more efficient than using the water buffalo, and we would become a more modern village.' 'But,' another elder countered, 'we would then have to generate money to buy petroleum.' 'And,' added another, 'some of the people of the village would not have work.' In the end, they decided *not* to buy a tractor." As I understood Api's translation, their reasoning was that everyone was currently working and eating, living and loving. They had no designs on conquering the next village. Their conclusion was that a tractor had more potential for damaging the fabric of their community than for developing it.

While several of the conditions for sustainability are met within this second story, we can focus again on the power of *meeting* just one: the opportunity for everyone to contribute and to be appreciated in return. It brought purpose and integrity to their community life.

Moving the frame closer to home, Gary Zukav offers a provocative view of what business might look like if seen in a whole new way. In a recent article entitled "Evolution and Business," Zukav asks, "What if the business of business was the evolution of the souls in it?" Toward the end of his article, he observes:

> *As the health of the environment, reverence for life, and appreciation of the earth as a living organism in a living Universe become integral to the orientation of business, business will become a natural champion of all that it now exploits—employees, customers, vendors, host communities, the environment, and the earth…a source of fulfillment to all who participate in it and a blessing to all who are touched by it.*

Focusing even more specifically, we can explore the individual leader's walk through the forest, elaborated in "Part II: The Path." We support evolutionary processes by developing our deeper and fuller personal powers which assist us in creatively connecting to a large source. This path of *powers to* that I am suggesting is only one path among many in the forest. It is drawn from a variety of ancient and modern spiritual freedoms: Buddhist and Christian thought, the seven chakras of Hinduism, the Jewish mystical Kabbalah, Native American traditions, and visionary colleagues. Through developing these powers we can bring balanced and coherent whole selves, including soul and spirit, to the world of work and recognize our work and our leadership roles as sacred.

I ponder the work and lives of Nelson Mandela, Gandhi, Mother Theresa, the Dalai Lama, Marianne Williamson, Martin Luther King, Barbara Marx Hubbard, and many others. What do they have in common that is so remarkably uncommon? In many ways, they all are just like you and me. They must eat and sleep; they have feelings, thoughts, and experiences they must make sense of. What then is unique about them? Have they, as Williamson said, overcome the fear of being "powerful beyond measure?" They all appear to recognize their life's work as sacred, and to see the importance of doing it in the world as the world is today, in order to make it into more of what they would like it to be tomorrow. All have clearly integrated individual spirituality deeply into their work. None felt it necessary, or even desirable, to check the deepest parts of her or himself at the doors of their workplaces.

At all levels—global, business, and individual—it is a "change of mind" that will bring a new garden into being. We are engaged in an evolutionary shift no less profound than to the one sea animals experienced when they emerged onto land and needed to replace gills with lungs. Zukav describes it as a shift from the five physical senses of seeing, hearing, tasting, touching, and smelling, to valuing and using many more senses. Like lungs seemed to fish, some of the additional senses are subtle and still seem out of reach. Yet, as Harman writes in *Global Mind Change*, "Imagine yourself a historian looking back from some time in the next century. What do you judge the most important thing that happened for the world in the twentieth century? My guess is that it will be something as quiet as a change of mind, a change of mind that is bubbling up out of the unconscious depths, spreading around the world, changing everything."

Organizations Are Agreements

I've forgotten what Western it comes from, but the line stays fresh in my mind. As his ranch is being repossessed, a cowpoke laments, "It's the Shawnee Cattle Company that's takin' it." Another rancher asks, "Who?" The first responds, "Ain't nobody. It's a company."

Ain't nobody. Our business organizations are not entities of substance within themselves. They do not rule themselves or us. They are not able to take responsibility for themselves. Rather, they reflect us and result from the agreements we make. Even if they were developed before we came along, they represent the agreements we continue to make and maintain. If we change our agreements, our organizations change.

Everything can change when there is an unwillingness to keep old agreements coupled with a desire to create new ones.

The unprecedented shift taking place in Eastern Europe has changed agreements and, thus, organizations—and it occurred with little or no bloodshed. The fall of the Berlin Wall demonstrated what happens when legitimacy is removed from institutions and those who lead them. Everything can change when there is an unwillingness to keep old agreements coupled with a desire to create new ones. Though the example is political, the same principles apply to business. As we consciously change our minds, as we deliberately embark on our spiritual journeys, and as our business organizations follow by becoming sources of support for life and growth, the garden of our planetary system will also change.

Chapter 6

Bridge People

The familiar life horizon has been outgrown, the old concepts, ideals and emotional patterns no longer fit, the time for the passing of a threshold is at hand.

—Joseph Campbell
Hero with a Thousand Faces

We Form a Link
Drawing on Ancient Wisdom
Sifting for Essence

We Form a Link

For his book *The Overview Effect: Space Exploration and Human Evolution*, Frank White interviewed twenty-four astronauts and cosmonauts to explore how their experiences had affected their perceptions of themselves, the world, the future—and, by extension, how their experiences have affected many of the rest of us. He uses a parable of fish to describe how he sees the natural yet profound evolutionary role space exploration is serving.

He asks us to imagine the world of a fish: the liquid water with vague distinctions of light and dark and, perhaps, a dim awareness of the ocean floor. Once in a while a fish may leap out of its water world and experience "something else." What White calls "fish consciousness" is limited by the fish's restricted physical world. A fish doesn't know what land is like—let alone sky. White then imagines what an enormous change it must have been for a fish to crawl onto land. The fish would be able to see "ocean" for the first time and see it as part of something much larger. How would this "explorer fish" explain "land" to other fish—with its different colors, sounds, views, textures, and solidness—once back in the water? White imagines the following dialogue:

"'Amazing,' they might say. 'That is quite incredible and rather brave of you to have risked it.' Some might not have been so charitable. 'Yes,' they might have said, 'very interesting, but how is it relevant to our lives here in the sea? What good is this 'land' to us?'" (p. 8)

Parallel to the parable, astronaut Rusty Schweickart described it this way: "Now you're out there and there are no frames, there are no limits, there are no boundaries.... You know very well at that moment, and it comes through to you so powerfully, that you're the sensing element for [humankind]." (White, p. 12)

The profound reflections and insights of astronaut and cosmonaut "explorer fish" have resulted in creative new organizations where we all can explore the changes occurring. An exemplary one is the Institute of Noetic Sciences in Sausalito, California, initiated by *Apollo 14* astronaut Edgar Mitchell. IONS has added much to our understandings of human consciousness through its exploration of non-traditional sciences such as healing and the mind-body connection, creative altruism, and paranormal experiences.

A period of transition attends transformative change. Transition times confront us with a welter of massive unknowns, chaos, and potential for human suffering. We can reduce the potential suffering by becoming more aware that we are in transition and by making choices that support our evolution rather than resist it. In other words, the more aware we are—and the more of us who are aware—the easier the transition will be. Becoming more conscious of our experiences *in* life and more awake to the sacredness of our contribution *to* life, makes us into "bridge people." We form the link between what has been and what is becoming.

> *We form the link between what has been and what is becoming.*

Although the astronauts may be the only humans leaving the earth physically, metaphorically they are not the only fish leaving the sea to explore new land. It takes a lot of strength, trust, tenacity, and courage to leave the sea and explore land. It also takes that combination of genius to return to the sea knowing that our evolution is inevitable. As bridge people, we look for ways to describe land, to give credence and validity to life both on land and in the sea, and to assure other fish that gills can become lungs in time. We encourage the shift from gills to lungs even as it appears we might die from lack of what we need to "breathe."

Drawing on Ancient Wisdom

A bridge connects one side with another. It is bidirectional rather than unidirectional. It is the same with us. We link ancient and emerging wisdom. For example, by exploring ancient principles of living in harmony with the earth, we can see the garden in a "new" way—not because the principles are new, but rather because they are an ancient remembering rekindled.

One set of ancient principles is the Native American tradition of the "Two Sacred Laws." In the Native American Council process, described further in Chapter 11, a community gathers wisdom and makes decisions together. Wisdom grows from hearing many perspectives around a circle, known as The Medicine Wheel. As any wheel is incomplete without its hub, the wisdom collected is incomplete without its connecting core principles. These two principles, or sacred laws, live at the center, known as The Children's Fire. Each question, idea, or proposal, with all of its wisdom gathered, is held to the crucible of the fire and tested against the two principles.

The two principles are:

1. A respect for natural processes of birth and growth; a respect for gestation. This principle includes, but encompasses far more than, human gestation, birth and growth. It signifies a respect for all newborns, from coyotes to ideas, as well as for natural life cycles, for the birthing processes of all life, and for the continuum of life—past, present, and future.

2. No decision is made, nothing is created or enacted, that can harm the children—both born and yet to be born. Again, this principle includes, but encompasses far more than, human children. It also accounts for plant "children," animal children, work-team children, creative-idea children, newly-emerging-thought and tool children—all children.

A respect for natural processes of birth and growth. Nothing is created or enacted that can harm the children.

The Two Sacred Laws

The Two Sacred Laws lay out concisely, first, *what* we are to do; and, second, *how* we are to do it. In other words, the first describes what we are responsible for: all that is born and has life. The second describes how we can meet our responsibility: by only enacting decisions that support and serve life in all stages of development and, conversely, making no decision that harms life.

These two principles are the very foundation for the successful evolution of life. They are simple enough for children to remember, and yet exquisitely elegant because they serve as a filter for covering complex territory. They become the basis for behavior and action, and thus the basis for creating present and future reality. These two principles have potential for helping leaders in business reorder priorities to fit into the natural laws and cycles of nature.

I shared them with my close friend and colleague, Peter. He is, among other things, a master of simplicity; naturally, I thought he'd really appreciate them. Instead his first response was to want to add complexity. He said, "But surely there must be more than two. I mean, what about what all the other cultures of the world bring, not to mention the modern world?"

"What else is there than what's contained in these two laws?" I asked. "Granted, Native American culture and tradition is not the only one that has this wisdom. It is universal and basic. Just like the golden rule of the Christian tradition: 'Do unto others as you would have them do unto you.' It appears, just worded differently, in every religion in the world. For example, in Buddhism it can be found as, 'Hurt not others in ways that you yourself would find hurtful.' In Hinduism it is 'Do naught unto others what would cause you pain if done to you.' But can you think of what else needs to be included here?"

He was stumped and became reflective. After a few moments, he said, "In looking at my own internal process, I notice I carry an assumption that our Western, highly technical culture must have something additional, something important, or something new to add. Actually, as I think about it, maybe it's the opposite. Perhaps The Two Sacred Laws represent what's been missing for us that has led us to this time of such seemingly overwhelming problems."

Sifting for Essence

We are in a time of shifting paradigms, changing perceptions of our world, dramatically evolving consciousness. As bridge people, one of our tasks is to sift everywhere for essence, meaning, and guidance. We must access the ancient and the emerging; face into the dark and bask in the light; let what is outside in, and what is inside out; live in this very moment while simultaneously considering seven generations to come; know that what we do "here" has ripple effects everywhere; play our individual parts while always being aware of the framework of a larger whole. It is complex. Were it not, we would find it easier to do.

Sift everywhere for essence, meaning, and guidance.

You can visualize the changes occurring as a series of inter-locking circles. An area the shape of a crescent moon is being shed from an initial circle. A second circle blends with what remains of the first and is larger because the potential of what is emerg-ing and evolving is greater than what has existed until now. Another new circle intersects and overlaps the first and second circles causing new crescent parts of them to be shed while it merges with what remains. And so on. Critical to these interlock-ing circles is the area of overlap. This intersect provides connection between past and future. But more, it provides grounding spiritually and emotionally in the same way that grav-ity grounds us physically.

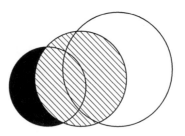

Interlocking Circles

How, you might ask, can you best play your individual part while always being aware of the framework of the larger whole? How can you activate a change of mind within yourself? The best possibility is within your grasp: your opportunity to deepen your individual power through your journey toward wholeness as a human being.

Part II

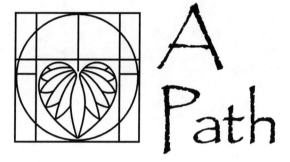

A
Path

PRELUDE

Walking a Path

I have always known
that at last I would take this road,
but yesterday I did not know
that it would be today.

—Narihara

Holding Up the Sun
Awareness of the Journey

Holding Up the Sun

In his tale *The Storyteller*, Peruvian writer Mario Vargas Llosa writes of an Amazonian tribe he calls the Machiguenga. The Machiguenga are nomadic, walking throughout the deep rain forest of eastern Peru. Their walking is imbued with deep meaning. They must walk because, in their belief system, their walking ensures that the sun will continue to rise into the sky; if they stop, the sun will fall, leaving all life in a world of darkness.

Throughout Part I two motifs surface again and again that parallel the Machiguenga's walking: looking for and challenging assumptions, and accessing more creativity to think anew. The sun we walk to hold up is the establishment, a global context that respects and supports life.

How is your walk imbued with deep meaning?

Consider your own walk through the forest. How is your walk imbued with deep meaning? What does your walking contribute to maintaining light in the world?

Part II is a path along which you can explore more about your walk, why you do it, and how you might strengthen it—a path of eight powers that are already available to you. Continuously walking through the forest is its own destination. By paying attention and deliberately choosing where and how you walk, you can find, clarify, and ripen new depths of these eight powers. Through maturing your capacity to access them, you acquire both the discernment and creativity necessary to better play your part in the unfolding drama of global transformation.

Deeper development of the eight powers allows you to take more advantage of the fullness for which you are designed, to draw on more of the potential naturally available to you.

Through developing these powers you will see the forest more fully, and experience the walk in even more wonderful ways than you have up to now. You will find ways, for example, to attend to more with less: more service with less energy, more creativity with less effort, more achievement with less time.

Part II is a path and not, by any means, the only path. A forest has many paths. Although I am using different language to describe the journey, aspects of this path have been walked in many different ways for many thousands of years, as Chapter 15 will hint at in more depth. The foundation that connects and integrates the eight powers is both ancient and eclectic.

While presented here in a linear fashion, these powers form a continuum. They are like the colors of the rainbow. Each color is indeed distinct, having its own particular energy, hue, and value; but there is also an area where the distinctions between adjoining colors melt into each other. Breaking the spectrum of wholeness into separate powers is only useful as a way to talk about them. They are not discrete; only blended together are they whole.

Awareness of the Journey

A forest changes and evolves. It is natural. We also change and evolve. One special "piece of equipment" that we have on our walk is awareness that we are aware. We can use consciousness to our advantage. Though we may walk the "same" path, for each of us it is different. I am perhaps captured by the beauty of the bright orange and purple mushrooms popping out of the vibrant green moss. I know no proper names for them. You may focus on the birds, knowing the cedar waxwing from the scarlet tanager; or perhaps you are taken by the sunlight playing on the leaves high up as the breeze lightly buffets them to and fro. Yet we walk in the same forest.

As you walk this suggested path with me, the powers are unfolded through my map and sight: my memories and recollections, my judgments and values, my hopes and desires. What

I see and experience as I walk the path is only a fraction of all that's there to be to be seen and experienced.

It was 8:30 on a clear, cool morning as I swung my day pack onto my back and locked the car door, up for another full day of walking through the back country of the redwood forest park. The sun was bright and the air was clear as I walked across the smooth asphalt parking lot. Suddenly, much to my surprise, I was lying flat on my back—well, actually, flat on my pack. Driving by, a park ranger stopped his truck, got out, and walked over to me, as I lay stunned but unhurt. "Tell me," he asked. "Exactly, how did this happen?" I didn't quite know how to respond. "I've hiked about fifty miles through the forest this week and I haven't fallen once," I said, "—until now." I looked down to see what had "caused" my fall; there lay the offending peach pit. Then I realized the reason I'd not noticed this hazard: "Actually, I wasn't paying attention, as I do on the trails, because I wasn't really hiking yet. I was on my way to hike." The true cause of my fall was not the peach pit but rather my lack of awareness of walking at that moment.

Consider taking time before you read each chapter to explore your thoughts about each power for yourself. Pay attention to your walking before you formally begin to read—while you are in the parking lot. Some reflective time can provide an opportunity for you to become more aware of what each power means to you, of what aspects of the forest you focus on. Questions for reflection precede each chapter in Part II. Use them if they are helpful, or use your own favorite means of contemplation. What you use doesn't matter. The point is to access your own knowing, to gather your own readiness.

Even though you and I may never meet, we "walk" together through Part II—I, through having written personally of my walk on this path, and you, through exploring it for yourself with me.

APATH I

Walking Within

While all eight powers originate from within, the root of the first four powers is different from that of the second four. The first four are rooted in your *internal conversation;* with them, you make inner meaning in your life. These powers are your grounding. They provide and develop your strength, purpose, clarity, and uniqueness. These powers are:

The Power of Aliveness
The Power of Passion
The Power of Integrity
The Power of Authenticity

Chapter 7

The Power of Aliveness

The most simple things in life are the most difficult things. Just getting through a day well is not easy. The most difficult thing in life, I think, is living. I mean really living.

—R.D. LAING

Questions for Reflection

1. What ideas come to your mind when you think of "Aliveness?"

2. What are some memories of when you felt especially alive?

3. How does aliveness support you in your walk and your work?

4. As a leader, what would you like to draw upon more within your aliveness?

5. At this moment, where are you taking a step of growth in your power of aliveness?

Letting Go
Engaging Fully
Presence and Attention
Safety and Security

Letting Go

It was the darkest time of winter. I was facing the most difficult time in the fifteen years of my consulting career in terms of both finance and identity. My second house in as many years was up for sale in order to "downsize" again. I was also feeling deeply uncertain about whether we *can* create a viable future; whether business leaders will claim their special role; whether we can change our thinking and our direction fast enough. It was a time of grief and despair, for myself and for all of life. Yet, poignantly, I felt alive.

To be fully alive means more than to survive; it means to thrive. Thriving is far more than success as conventionally defined: a continuous ascent. To the contrary; in *The Heart Aroused*, David Whyte writes,

> *[the] extent to which we exclude the shadowy, failing sides of our-*
> *selves from the workplace is the extent to which one half of us is*
> *hidden… We think we exist only when our life looks like the first*
> *half of the cycle, when our sense of ourselves is growing and get-*
> *ting larger, when we are succeeding or stepping up to the line for*
> *promotion. If things are dying or falling away, we dismiss it, we*
> *refuse to see it as the second half of the very same cycle and think*
> *there is something "wrong" with us.* (pp. 284-285)

The alternative to noticing the shadowy parts is denial. There are circumstances in which denial is a saving grace, a means of getting through difficult or seemingly impossible circumstances. But denial of common, everyday life consumes energy, saps vitality, and dampens emotion. Being completely alive, with full-ness of energy, vitality, and emotion, can be difficult at times. It means facing into incidents and conditions you might rather not see. When you finally do see them and recognize that they belong to you, you must own them. Being fully alive and choos-ing to be directly in your life may sometimes mean feeling lost and vulnerable. There are costs to being fully alive.

While that dark winter time in my life could be seen as "fail-ure," I have come to see it as one of the most successful times of my life—because I learned so much. Some of the lessons were new, while others were another turn of the spiral of ongoing life lessons. I learned that great riches come from letting others in to really see me and support me; that receiving, connecting, and being able to be vulnerable are gifts more blessed than any of my other achievements.

Also, the impact of these lessons was deepened *through expe-rience*, through coming to understand them in my gut, having "known" them only intellectually before. For example, I in-tellectually understood that events are neutral; that meaning comes from my interpretation; that I decide on the "goodness" or "badness" of what occurs. The gift of this time was learning the truth of this truth emotionally.

One day, when things were at their hardest, I noticed myself more at peace than I had been on the previous day. Externally nothing had changed. I still was selling my house, I still had no prospect for immediate income, I still knew that some people might think me a failure. What had changed? Simply put, the change had taken place not in my circumstances, but instead in my attitude and my interpretation of what was occurring in my life. I felt the direct consequence of letting go. I had known about the power of letting go, but had a difficult time understanding how to *do* it. It is especially difficult to move from the mere knowl-edge to the experience of letting go, because "doing" letting go is a paradox. Witnessing myself while in the midst of letting go was a great relief; it increased my aliveness tremendously.

Letting go allowed me to have my human "beingness" in new ways, especially as a professional businesswoman. I had to change my limited belief that competence equals busyness and income. Learning and growth came from noticing that I have been and still am successful—both through expanding my definition of success and through letting go of what success had been to me up until then. The less concern I felt about my professional identity, the more I experienced willingness and ability to speak vulnerably about the conditions of my life.

A measure of my pain was coming from what my colleague, Debashis, calls "suffering by comparison." It goes like this: If you don't know something exists, you probably don't need it and don't suffer from wanting it even if you could have it. I watch my son, Michael, who is in kindergarten this year. For the first time he's watching advertising on commercial television at his before and after-school daycare "mom's" house. As Christmas approached, his language became more and more peppered with "I want..." and "Can you add this toy to the list?" Michael is originally from the Amazon region of Peru. If he still lived in the village of his ancestors, he wouldn't know Lego Systems, Power Rangers, or Micro Machines existed. He wouldn't suffer by comparison for lack of them. While his enchantment might be more blatant and unreserved than mine, I am often equally trapped in my own suffering by comparison, as the story of "my" Mercedes and Russian sable coat will illustrate in Chapter 8.

In this case, in the darkness of winter, I saw my colleagues having full work calendars and receiving attendant rewards. I suffered by comparison from having neither at that moment. When I let the comparisons go and let people more fully into my life, what I received instead was support, compassion, and empathy. For example, one person experiencing ascent even shared the story of a past bankruptcy.

I learned—and I survived! I have come out the other side with more calm and more acceptance of myself. I am more real, in the way Margery Williams has the toy horse describe "real" to the stuffed rabbit in her classic story *The Velveteen Rabbit*:

It doesn't happen all at once. You become. It takes a long time. That's why it doesn't often happen to people who break easily, or have sharp edges, or who have to be carefully kept. Generally, by the time you are Real, most of your hair has been loved off, and your eyes drop out and you get loose in the joints and very shabby. But these things don't matter at all, because once you are Real you can't be ugly, except to people who don't understand. (p. 5)

Engaging Fully

Having a life and *living* a life are significantly different. The phrase "earning a living" is used as a synonym for "working for money." Through that idiom we subtly come to believe we must earn our lives. We do not have to earn a *living*; we are already *alive*. Life is a gift given to us. Living your life, really entering into it, demonstrates the extent to which you claim the gift *you* have been given.

Having *a life and* living *a life are significantly different.*

Many years ago, I slowly ambled through an exhibit called "The Continuum." It crossed over disciplines, through time, and beyond conventional boundaries. Some of the concepts were new to me and affected me deeply. I viewed an exhibit on death and dying that included videotape of Elizabeth Kubler-Ross conversing with terminally-ill children about how they released fear and accepted what was happening to them.

Next came a series of panels on near-death experiences. One was a painting of the "tunnel of light," near a display containing the words of people who had undergone near-death experiences. For example, one person had "died" on an operating table and witnessed the activity in the operating room from above. In that moment, she found she had a choice—to go into the tunnel, or to return to her body. Realizing she had more to do here on the earth, she decided not to go toward the light yet, though it was tempting.

As I turned from that panel, I came face to face with a hologram of a woman's head and shoulders. Viewed from one side, she leaned forward and ran her fingers through her hair; from the other side, she lifted her chin and leaned her head back as if to moan or weep in grief, despair, and rage. I saw myself—alive, but without joy. In that moment I made a conscious decision that was twofold: to do whatever was necessary, within my capacity, not to die prematurely; and to become more fully alive.

Paradoxically, being fully alive means being prepared to die at any moment.

Paradoxically, being fully alive means being prepared to die at any moment. While working in The Sudan with arriving Ethiopian refugees during the heavily publicized famine of the mid-eighties, I had an opportunity to take a short "vacation" in Ethiopia. I wanted to see where people came from and how they made their journey. To reach the regions I wanted to visit, I had to fly. As I walked onto the tarmac in Addis Ababa I discovered, to my dismay, an old DC-3. Smiling when he saw my shock, the agent said, "In your country, you can only see such planes in the Smithsonian." I observed my feet moving me toward the old aircraft as I wondered what I was doing. Once on board I noticed small corroded spots where I could see through to fresh air. With momentary panic and shortness of breath, I considered getting off. What stopped me was my desire to see and feel my experience of that time more deeply. As we took off I distinctly remember thinking, "This is a good day and a good way to die."

Presence and Attention

Safety and security are often assumed to come from stable conditions—keeping things as they are. But the constant condition is change, not sameness. Another quality that influences aliveness is how well you relate to change and transition. If you resist and try to control change in your life, you suffer. Aliveness means becoming skilled at riding the waves of change, and learning to love the ride.

The change we are most familiar with involves moving from one known state to another known state—from individual contributor to manager, from being single to being married. While this change may *feel* transformational when it involves you, it is change that has been witnessed and experienced by others before you.

Transformative change differs significantly from change-as-usual. Its most distinctive feature is that we cannot predict the outcome while we are in the midst of it. During transformative change we move from a known state to an as-yet-unknown, entirely new state. Something new is being born. You may have learned that it is beneficial and a sign of leadership competence to be in control—or, at least, to behave as though you are in control. Yet, if the outcome is unknown, how is it possible to be in control? What is it you will be in control of? Times of transformative change can be frightening.

Barbara Marx Hubbard offers the analogy of a baby in the womb. Imagine the unborn saying, "It's getting too crowded in here, there's not enough space, I'm going to die!" just before it is time for birth. The baby can no longer stay in the womb. Natural law requires it to transform into an entirely different state by traveling through the birth canal. Herein lies a paradox of birth: it is common and required of us all, yet at the same time profoundly transformative.

Perhaps the disintegrating systems of our time can be seen as the womb that has nourished us this far—but which we have outgrown. Perhaps what feels like an ever-increasing amount of chaos is the newness of passing through the birth canal to a newness of such magnitude that it is redefining what it means to be human.

Perhaps every generation thinks its times are uniquely transformative; perhaps they are. Perhaps our times aren't. Who knows? But why miss out, given the possibility? In any case, choosing daily to live as though these are time of birth and transformation increases aliveness. We become midwives attending the miracle of birth.

Passing through the birth canal is a transition time fraught with fear from losing the familiar, attended by a sense of chaos from not knowing what is coming. In *Surviving Corporate Transitions*, William Bridges writes,

> *Change occurs when something new starts or something old stops, and it takes place at a particular point in time. But transition cannot be localized in time that way, since it is the gradual...process through which individuals and groups reorient themselves. Change often starts with a new beginning, but transition must start with an ending—with people letting go of old attitudes and behaviors.*

A gift of the birth canal is that it demands our full presence and attention. No matter how much we might struggle, we cannot re-enter the womb. We can only be where we are and what we are at that moment. In writing about "The Law of Least Effort" in *The Seven Spiritual Laws of Success*, Deepak Chopra says, "Flowers don't try to bloom. They bloom. Birds don't try to fly. They just fly." And he adds, "When you struggle against this moment, you're actually struggling against the entire universe." That's a lot to struggle against.

The completion of the quote from R.D. Laing that opened this chapter is particularly appropriate here: "A lot of the time I'm in the present, and I'm thinking about the past or scheming about the future and missing every present moment, instead of actually partaking of the sacrament of every present moment."

Safety and Security

In spite of feeling lonely, fatigued, and scared, I head off into the Somali desert with four men I only know well enough to have decidedly mixed feelings about. As we drive west out of Mogadishu the sky is the eternal blue of the end of the hot season before the rains. Our destination is Luuq, a town on the border with Ethiopia. Luuq, I'm told, holds the distinction of being in the *Guinness Book of World Records* for having the hottest average daily temperature of any place on the planet. There are hotter places, but Luuq is the hottest on average. I come from the north, and I don't particularly like heat. I wonder how will I do.

Tens of thousands of Ethiopian refugees live in camps around Luuq. As staff of a management development project we are going to where they live to learn how we can best support the camp administrators. And, as long as I find myself in this strange and incomprehensible place, I want to see some of the region.

After four hours of driving we leave the tarmac. The going becomes slower. We are on a dirt track that looks as though it goes off into nowhere—and it does. There may have been some variation in the land, but, if so, it was too subtle for my eyes. What if we got lost? Hours go by. At one point the track splits into three. "Hussein, how do you know which track leads to Luuq?" I ask. He responds, "Any of the three will do. They're all made by UN food trucks and the only place to go out here is Luuq." We finally see the settlement looming magically on the horizon like a mirage.

On this particular evening there is no electricity. There used to be, but the town's generator has been broken for months. Many people sleep in hammocks; at night the heat of the day rises up out of the earth and to be higher means to be cooler. Darkness near the equator comes suddenly and completely at about 6:00 P.M. and much of the "day" occurs outside after dark. I hear what I cannot see. People walk and talk, children play, onions fry, the wheels of a donkey cart squeak, dogs bark. These sounds on a small, local scale mingle with the strange quiet of no traffic, radios, or televisions.

I am in awe. Where am I? Am I still on the same planet as my loved ones back home? I'm ten hours by car from Mogadishu and two hours from there by plane to Nairobi. But the planes only fly three times a week. So how far am I *really* from emergency medical care? To put a telephone call through to the United States from Mogadishu could take days—but at least there the possibility exists. Here it's impossible. As I climb into my hammock at night, I consider how I'm out of touch with the world as I know it and as it knows me.

Once settled and gently rocking, I look up. I see stars in the blackest of skies. So many stars! As I gaze, I remember, as a fourteen-year-old, standing alone on a cold winter night in rural northern Minnesota waiting for the bus to take me to a high-school basketball game. While waiting, I stamped my feet to stay warm, looked up into the night sky and picked out all of the constellations I knew. Here in Luuq, where everything is so alien and unfamiliar, I see something familiar: constellations of stars in the rural darkness of a night sky. A sense of safety washes over me. That moment defined paradox for me. I was as far from "safety" as I had ever been and yet I was safe. I slept.

Being fully alive means experiencing safety day to day by losing fear and gaining trust; deciding for yourself what security is and how success looks; letting go of what holds you back; and choosing to fully engage in the gift that is your life.

Chapter 8

The Power of Passion

What in your life is calling you?
When all noise is silenced,
the meetings adjourned,
the lists laid aside,
& the wild iris blooms by itself
in the dark forest
what still pulls on your soul?

—from *The Box: Remembering the Gift*

Questions for Reflection

1. What ideas come to your mind when you hear "Passion?"

2. What are some memories of times you felt especially passionate?

3. How does passion support you in your walk and your work?

4. As a leader, what would you like to draw upon more within your passion?

5. At this moment, where are you taking a step of growth in your power of passion?

Deep Meaning
The *Via Negativa*
Staying on Purpose

Deep Meaning

Think back, for a moment, on times when you were involved in something very dear to your heart and lost track of everything except what you were doing. Times when, no matter what others felt or said, you remained on the path you were following. Times when, after hard work that was important to you, you had more rather than less energy. When you felt like a sponge, absorbing everything you could—and then still wanted to learn more. When you were so engaged it felt like it had as a child, playing with abandon, creativity, and verve.

You are the only person who can empower you.

The memories that come to your mind are indicators of passion and purpose in your life. They denote aspects of your reason for being, and are examples of what it means for you to be empowered. These days, "empower" is commonly used in organizations to mean drawing more from others—as in "we need to more fully empower our employees." But this is impossible. You are the only person who can empower you. Empowerment comes from within: drawing out the best, the most, the fullest, the deepest of who you are and who you can be. The most anyone else can do is to provide a nourishing, supportive, creative environment for you.

Delving more deeply into your personal reason for being and deciding to act as fully as possible in concert with your higher purpose can serve as an antidote, a medicine, for moving beyond pain or denial. Whenever you find yourself feeling despair, reconnecting with your dream can be a source of great comfort and deep meaning. You may or may not have touched your personal dream yet. Exploring *your* dream may require courage. Pressure to walk the path approved by our culture can feel enormous: be practical, acquire material comforts, have more than enough. The pressure is, if anything, even more intense in the worlds of work and career: be serious and conservative, keep dreams and passion private. Yet unveiling the lightness and audacity of your dreams and passion leads to greater fulfillment and greater riches, exciting breakthroughs and new dreams.

Alignment with your purpose aids you in making common decisions uncommonly well, in having uncommon impact while engaging in common actions.

The Via Negativa

To touch your dream in a different way, notice what you have said no to. As David Whyte writes in *The Heart Aroused*, "The *via negativa* is the discipline of saying no when we have as yet no clarity about those things to which we can say *yes*... In the continuous utterance of the *no* is a profound faith that the yes will appear...*because* we have said *no* to so much." It sometimes means saying "no" to what may appear a great opportunity to everyone else—but would, in your own discernment, ultimately be a diversion for you, consuming your energy and diffusing your focus.

Saying "no" may result in temporarily living with less income, less certainty, less illusion of control; temporarily living at the edge of despair until the truly appropriate next leg of the journey is revealed. Describing breakthrough or transformation in *The Book of Runes*, Ralph Blum writes, "In each life there comes at least one moment which, if recognized and seized, transforms the course of that life forever. Rely, therefore, on radical trust, even though the moment may call for you to leap, empty-handed, into the void."

I had successfully completed my second year as a consultant. Following work with a corporation on the East Coast, I went to

Brattleboro, Vermont, to visit old friends. While telling each other stories of our lives, Don said, "You want stories? We can give you stories. We're currently staffing a management development project in Somalia. Are you interested?" I laughed, "Well, now, there's the end of the world! But, don't tempt me. I have been feeling bored."

Two weeks later, while consulting in greater Los Angeles, I was struck by the opulence of some areas: the sizes of the homes with the high fences and gates around them, the number of Porsches, BMWs, and Jaguars on the freeways. I imagined having more of what I was seeing. Specifically, I wanted a Mercedes coupe and a Russian sable coat. At the rate my business was growing, it wouldn't be too long before I could give myself those symbols of success.

One evening I saw the film *Gandhi* and was inspired by the wisdom and the simplicity portrayed in the title character. I was struck by the depth and consistency of purpose Gandhi developed over a lifetime; and by the impact he, as one human being, had—and continues to have. When called a visionary, his response was, "I am not a visionary. I am a practical idealist." I left the theater changed. From my hotel room I called my Vermont colleagues and said, "Okay, I'm ready to talk about Somalia."

Six weeks later, uncertain about whether I would ever return to it, I suspended my consulting practice. I rented my home, packed my bags, said good-bye to loved ones, and boarded a plane for Frankfurt, Rome, and Mogadishu.

Purpose in my life grew from an ember to a flame. I do not have, nor have I ever had, a Mercedes coupe or a Russian sable coat. What I have instead is greater clarity about my purpose and how to express it. For today, I see my purpose as participating in the positive shaping of the fundamental global transformation through discovering my personal power, deepening my leadership capacity, walking my spiritual path, parenting, writing, participating in like-minded communities, offering service to organization-change projects, and engaging with corporate business leaders.

Staying on Purpose

Five years ago the time came for me to leave for Peru to meet Michael and finalize his adoption. Being both a sole proprietor and sole provider I planned carefully and fully, knowing I was taking on a great responsibility. I had been told I would be away two to four weeks; having some knowledge of Latin American bureaucracy, I planned for six weeks. Nothing worked as I had been told it would. After twelve weeks in Peru with no end in sight, I let my projects go, helping clients find other resources. I faced the temporary collapse of my consulting practice. I arrived home with an infant and time but no income.

I made only one decision: to stay on purpose. I worked hard to initiate the Minnesota Chapter of the World Business Academy, an organization aligned with my own vision for the role of business in the world. I wrote for publication for the first time in *When the Canary Stops Singing: Women's Perspectives on Transforming Business*. Though I had worries and fears about how to pay the bills, it was a deeply empowering time of my life.

It is not always easy to stay on purpose, to stay with your passion. It may seem impractical, inexpedient, or even unnecessary. Yet, Whyte gives a poignant example of one woman who noticed a divergence between her current life and her calling. She wrote:

> *Ten years ago…*
> *I turned my face for a moment*
> *and it became my life.*

The power of passion in leadership is rooted in the satisfaction and force that comes with finding deep spiritual meaning and purpose in your life—and, once you have found it, being willing to stay with it in spite of apparent hardship. Approaching your life through deep meaning is its own reward and sustenance.

Chapter 9

The Power of Integrity

Everything you meet
along the path
is yourself.

—Zen proverb

Do I contradict myself?
Very well then, I contradict myself,
(I am large, I contain multitudes).

—WALT WHITMAN, "SONG OF MYSELF"

Questions for Reflection

1. What ideas come to your mind when you hear "Integrity?"

2. What are some memories of times you felt a high degree of integrity?

3. How does integrity support you in your walk and your work?

4. As a leader, how would you like to draw on more of your integrity?

5. At this moment, where are you taking a step of growth in your power of integrity?

Personal Ethic

Courage

Congruence

Personal Ethic

Much of what *you* consider "right" or ethical is a result your culture, community, and family. In truth, much of what is ethical is relative rather than absolute because cultures themselves are relative.

Some friends tell the story of an ethical dilemma they faced while in the Peace Corps. A young boy seriously injured his leg with a machete. The local culture's ethical response, built up over millennia, was to send the boy away from the village to die; he could not survive the hardships of village life disabled, and others would suffer as well if they tried to care for both him and themselves. It was their way. My friends wanted to rush him on a many-hour journey to a city with a hospital. They couldn't stand by and watch an individual life be unnecessarily extinguished — no matter what the future might hold. It was *their* way.

But if they did get him to the hospital alive, the boy would most likely lose his leg. He would return to the village alive, but disabled. He would then be sent away. What to do? There was no right or wrong in absolute terms. There was only right and wrong in culturally relative terms.

Across cultures, judging what is ethical or "in integrity" can prevent the development of relationships or damage those that have been built. An everyday example of cultural relativity in global business is what we consider "under the table bribes." In some cultures this practice may not be considered unethical and, to the contrary, may be seen as practical and sensible, if only because people know it is happening and therefore expect it. The same principle of tacit agreement on what is considered ethical is exhibited in our own culture in the context of labor-management negotiations. Each side asks for more than they expect to get, knowing that they will have to relinquish some of their demands. It is not considered unethical because it is the way things work and everyone understands the rules.

Ethical "ground" can shift dramatically over time both within and across cultures.

Ethical "ground" can shift dramatically over time both within and across cultures. Remember back to when you were in school; getting help from another student was probably construed as cheating. Today, it's called teamwork. Students are encouraged to pool their knowledge and skill because we have come to deem such skills valuable in helping young people prepare for the emerging workplace environment.

Your personal ethic is just that: *your* personal ethic. Using your ethical base as a standard for judging the behavior and integrity of others, however, can lead to difficulty and disappointment. For example, I worked with an upper-level executive who, due to extreme disagreements, parted from his company. While providing support after the separation, I was struck by his apparent rigidity about what was "ethical." He related how his former colleagues were unethical, that they had no principles or integrity. It may have been an appropriate defense at the time, a way to justify what had happened and to survive the interim. But as was the case for him, exercising your own personal ethic to judge others can lead you into separation and isolation.

Living in other cultures can help you see the relativity of your culture's ethic. Life experiences help you identify your individual, personal ethical base. My awareness of my right and responsibility to determine my own personal ethic occurred while I was living in a Muslim culture. Islamic women were hidden from view. I was exempt from living by the rules of the culture, and as a Western woman, felt more free to do as I pleased than I had in the United States. For the first time in my life I could choose whether and how much I wanted to conform to the social norms. I actually had to consider my behaviors. For example, was I going to wear a mini-skirt and halter top to the Muslim market or cover myself as was considered appropriate—ethical—for Muslim women? I remember feeling really fantastic in discovering where I stood—minus the "shoulds" and "shouldn'ts" of my cultural ethic. I was my own authority and, through that freedom, I discovered the "bottom line" about what was right for me.

I continue to clarify my personal values and principles—and, thus, my ethical base—through how I define my business. How well I stay aligned with what I believe, and how gracefully I change as my beliefs change, mirrors how in integrity I am at any given time. For example, what criteria do I use for accepting one project over another? At least three different levels of "test" have arisen. Does it fit into my personal purpose and will I have an impact? Is it work that truly draws on *my* gifts and talents or would someone else be a better resource? Finally, when I'm ninety-five and sitting in a porch rocker watching the sunset, will I remember doing the work with joy or regret?

I make many mistakes, but usually not the same one more than once. Once I agreed to teach time management, which is outside my expertise, to a group of managers. The request came when I didn't have work and needed income, but it had nothing to do with my personal purpose and it didn't draw on my best skills and talents. It also didn't match my beliefs: I don't believe we *can* manage the construct we call "time." Time goes on. We only manage ourselves in relation to the apparent passing of time. The training wasn't a total failure, just amazingly mediocre. I doubt I had positive impact, and I was embarrassed. Though not necessarily useful for that company, it was a useful experience for me; I remember it vividly, and it continues to serve as a measure.

Ethics are relative. Integrity is finding and acting from your personal ethical base of values and principles. Your internal ethic is your guide for action in the world.

Courage

Coming to clearly know your own integrity provides spine. Your backbone holds you up. It allows you to stand firmly, wherever you stand. As my colleague Kaz said at a time when I was facing an ethical dilemma about whether and how to confront a sticky issue on a project, "When you stand for something, there are things you won't stand for."

You must know what you personally stand for, be willing to stand there, and clearly communicate where you stand.

As you lead in today's and tomorrow's world—with or without the power of position—strengthening your spine will help you take your stand. In order to do so, you must know what you personally stand for, be willing to stand there, and clearly communicate where you stand. You can only do that when you are certain inside yourself. Taking a stand can be risky. It calls for and requires courage.

"Courage" comes from the Old French word *curage*, meaning "having the mental or moral strength to venture, persevere, and withstand danger, fear, or difficulty." With courage you can venture with integrity into that which might be dangerous.

In business settings, risks are usually other than the kind required of firefighters facing a raging forest blaze, or the astronauts aboard the damaged *Apollo 13*. Risk in those situations carry life-or-death stakes. Risk in the workplace more often involves *perceived* threats. Perceptions of what we *think* might happen keep us from speaking our minds, asking why, or taking a stand. Confronting these entrenched, unspoken norms and assumptions takes awareness and courage.

I assisted a team in searching for high-leverage points that could help bring about fundamental change in their work processes. Although not specifically asked for, the ongoing conflict in their relationships consistently surfaced as an obstacle to high productivity during the preliminary interviews. One fault line of this conflict was between the co-managers and other team members. The others perceived their managers as having secrets because they saw the two whispering together frequently.

When the group confronted them, the managers were stunned that they appeared secretive. They disclosed that, in his staff meetings, *their* manager often prefaced his comments with, "This is not to leave this room." Respecting his request and wanting to do the right thing, they kept his secrets.

Of course, there are many things in organizations which, for a variety of reasons—including compassion—are kept confidential. "Is that the case in this instance?" I asked. "No," said one manager; "Well, some is and some isn't." The other manager continued, "I'd like to report everything to the staff. I think it would help us do our work better. But I've agreed to keeping stuff secret."

"Why have you agreed to keep it secret?" one team member asked.

There was no "good" answer. Both managers agreed that they didn't like what they were doing but both also said that they had not questioned it. They had assumed it went with the territory of managing in their environment.

I asked the team members, "When this 'confidential' information finally surfaces, is it news to you?" Their responses were an emphatic and unanimous no. One said, "The company grapevine is better than any other form of communication we have."

The next question was, "What would happen if you questioned your manager by asking why specific pieces of information need to be kept confidential?" Both managers groaned and palpable fear surfaced. They feared some unnamed punishment or loss for confronting authority. In truth, they were living amidst loss already: their separation from the rest of the group, and the impact it was having on everyone's ability to function fully. They decided they would risk. And the rest of us all saw the courage it would take to help their manager sift through the information he delivered.

Congruence

Integrity and courage help you follow your own spirit without hesitation. Being clear and confident in your own values and principles can have significant impact on the profitability and image of your business. There is something special—something extremely compelling and attractive—that surrounds a person or business grounded on a firm foundation of self-defined integrity. That something special is congruence. Integrity means knowing your deepest personal truth. Courage is how you put that truth out into the world. Congruence is matching integrity and courage, belief and behavior.

A particular form of predictability results from congruence. It contrasts with sameness or routine, because this predictability can be distinctly different from one situation to another; consistency is at the level of pattern rather than event. It is a correspondence between words and actions that we commonly call it "walking the talk." Many organizations try to "walk their talk," only to find themselves falling far short. If that is your experience, consider first learning to "talk your walk" through speaking about what *really* happens—even where it differs from what you wish. Articulating and revealing reality, "the walk," can be enlightening. You come to see the true nature of your collective actions and behaviors. Unless you truly stand in your talk, you cannot skillfully walk it.

A department was investigating whether their current structure matched the way they got work done. They called their structure "team-based." A small group researched team-based structures by visiting other organizations, conducting phone interviews, and reading the literature. In reporting back to a larger group, one said, "We may *say* we are team-based, but we are still organized as a hierarchy. You know," she went on, "I don't think it really matter *how* we're structured. What matters is that we get honest about it."

Congruence engenders trust. Internally, it engenders a self-trust and inspires a self-confidence very different from ego or arrogance. And, because of the internal trust, it also gives rise to trust in others. You may not recognize everyone you meet who is internally congruent, but you certainly can distinguish a person whose actions and words match from a person whose do not.

Being congruent allows you to know intimately and acknowledge those places where you are incongruent. Call it coming to know your "perfect imperfections." Congruence means embracing the whole of who you are, and allowing hidden parts of yourself to be revealed.

These days I get to practice "walking my talk" every day with my five-year-old son, Michael. The power of his truth coming back to me so directly is a mirror. Children are congruent they speak the truth and communicate with abandon—until they learn differently. They demonstrate that everything continually changes; that integrity and congruence are not firm and forever lines drawn in the sand. They provide consistent, powerful, and revealing feedback day after day, and provide reason for continually looking at where you stand.

So it is with the metaphoric children mentioned with The Two Sacred Laws first discussed in Chapter 6. In the business environment, if you listen, the children that can help you see whether you are congruent in walking your talk might include new organizations, new MBA graduates, college interns, people who transfer in, or a new venture group. As with children in a family, they are exquisitely able to see discrepancy, question why, and offer creative new ideas—unless or until they become so acculturated that they learn "it can't be done."

Chapter 10

The Power of Authenticity

Since our lives depend on it, we instinctively feel that the heart holds the essence of our being, the core of who we really are. Words, thoughts, and feelings that seem to come from there have a truth and power, a kind of sincerity that no others can match. Numerous folk sayings throughout the world attest to a widespread belief that the wisdom of the heart is somehow deeper and truer than the knowledge of the head.

—EDWIN BERNBAUM
The Way to Shambhala

Questions for Reflection

1. What ideas come to your mind when you hear "authenticity?"

2. What are some memories of times you felt especially authentic?

3. How does authenticity support you in your walk and your work?

4. As a leader, how would you like to draw on more of your authenticity?

5. At this moment, where are you taking a step of growth in your power of authenticity?

Self-Referral

Centering

Inner Peace

The power of authenticity comes from tapping into the well of your inner wisdom. Wisdom is the ability to discern inner qualities and relationships, to grasp your own insights. In other words, authenticity results from exploring what you *really* think more than rethinking from conditioning; discovering what you *really* feel over what you think you "should" feel; determining what you *really* need and perceiving what you *really* want.

Self-Referral

"Self-referral," Deepak Chopra says, means looking within yourself for evaluation and fulfillment. It is contrasted with "object-referral:" looking to others, experiences, situations, and things to establish your identity and define you and your worth. It is, in short, being victim—making yourself a victim—to the world outside of you.

Much of what is written for business audiences is impersonal and rational. Some is detached from the human condition. My writing is not detached, so my fear surfaces. In writing for a business audience, must I change both my writing style and my content? Or, if I continue to write through story, analogy, and experience, *and* claim to be writing for a business audience, might I be rejected? Conventional wisdom says that good business leaders exhibit objectivity, toughness, rationality, and a focus on solving problems "out there." Yet my writing says we *must* look "in here" for both the problems and the solutions. And whenever we go within, problems and solutions become subjective, personal, related to feelings, and spiritual.

A colleague called and related joyfully that he had read some of my writing and it touched him deeply. He said, "You write in the way I think and feel. It's freeing for me because I am planning to write. Until now I assumed my writing would have to be rational and abstract, since that's my experience of business writing." Then he added, "But who do you think will read this sort of business writing?"

Authentic means real, not imaginary, false, or imitation. Authenticity is personal truth in action. To write authentically, I write to and for the children. While they may never read my writing, they are my true audience. They are the beneficiaries who, in a non-linear sense, become the ultimate audience. I write easily *to* the children because they love a good story, especially one they've heard before. I write *for* the children because this is part of my life's legacy.

To concern myself with how an imagined, monolithic, "rational business audience" might judge my truth is intimidating; it quickly leads me to consider veiling what I have to say or, worse, to consider not saying it at all. Aiming toward a specific profile of readers has a number of virtues to commend it, including the ability to use appropriate language, an awareness of particular sensitivities, and finding examples easy to identify with. But aiming might also mean perpetuating assumptions that need exposure.

Centering

Establishing self-referral within yourself results from being centered. Learning to center comes naturally, as you can see when you watch a child learn to walk. It also happens over time, by learning how to "come home" to yourself. Daily practice, in whatever form suits you, both re-establishes and deepens your connection to yourself. One method of reaching into your center is sitting in stillness, in quiet. As Meister Eckhart observed in the thirteenth century: "Nothing in all creation is so like God as stillness."

I had heard of meditation some years before but was afraid of it. Being one who only touched the edges the 1960s revolution, I linked meditation to psychedelic drugs, communal living, rebellion, and other foreign concepts. Even more significant, I feared that in meditation I would go somewhere and not return; that I would lose control.

Stillness is our opportunity to listen.

Instead, meditation allows me to connect with myself as a day-to-day human being. Sitting in stillness gives me access to what the Quakers call "the still, small voice within." Thus, through sitting alone in stillness, I gain connection to my higher self, God, spirit, the great mystery, or however you describe a connectedness with everything. That still, small voice has many names; but it is still the same source. It speaks to each of us, within each of us, every day—whether or not we listen to it or appreciate it. Stillness is our opportunity to listen.

Another method of centering is through *moving* in stillness and quiet. One principle of the dance-like movements of *T'ai Chi Chu'an* is imagining the upper body moving gently, softly—in an airy manner, like the sky, clouds, and heaven—while imagining the lower body rooted deeply into the earth to provide stability and groundedness. The concentration required to move with precision brings my conscious attention into the present and, for a time, I let go of my past and future. I move differently, breathe differently, think differently.

Centering through stillness and quiet, in communion with the still, small voice within, can happen through your most common experiences: watching the morning sun shimmering on blue water, gazing at a perfect rosebud and smelling its delicious aroma, listening to music that moves you, staring into a fire, hearing rain on the roof, becoming one with your bed just before sleep comes. These all can be moments of deep connection and centeredness. Centering allows you to slow down enough to witness yourself living your life as you live it.

Inner Peace

During a household "archeological dig," my high-school gradu-ation picture surfaced. I propped it up on my desk. Near it was a current photo for a marketing mailing. I glimpsed both photos and was struck by the contrast. The high-school photo portrays me as sweetly pretty, with no facial wrinkles. My hair and cloth-ing are perfectly arranged. My smile appears gentle. Yet, I remember how anxious, uncertain, inadequate, insecure, and worried I felt inside. The current photo was taken in a rush between getting Michael to day care and making a meeting on time. I hurriedly put on a bit of make-up, tamed my hair, and adjusted my jacket while thinking, "Well, so be it!" The result-ing photo shows my wrinkles and imperfections. My smile is crooked but genuine, authentic to my happiness inside. These two photos mark a difference between object-referral and self-referral in my life. I still harbor the teenager within me, of course, but with more experience and tools to help me regain self-refer-ral when I am overcome by object-referral.

Authenticity is your source of great wisdom and creativity.

Authenticity is your source of great wisdom and creativity. It is also your "growing edge." What is authentic in you is like new leaves on a tree in spring—full of life and bursting with potential while, at the same time, tender and vulnerable.

Authenticity, through self-referral, centering, and finding peace, expresses your respect and love for yourself in ways far different from narcissism or self-absorption. The power of authenticity combines your powers of aliveness, passion, and integrity in order to bring forth the best of who you are. Authenticity expresses your relationship to yourself, bringing you to new readiness for depth and service in your relationships and connections with the world beyond you.

A PATH II

Walking With

The first four powers, as noted earlier, are rooted in your internal conversation. The second four powers are rooted in your *interactions* with all of life and in the reality you witness outside of yourself. They apply the meaning you establish with the first four powers. These powers are your declaration in the world. They give voice and action to your strength, purpose, clarity, and uniqueness through relationship, creativity, outlook, and awe. These powers are:

The Power of Relatedness
The Power of Expression
The Power of Perspective
The Power of Reverence

Chapter 11

The Power of Relatedness

I tried to know myself.
From within, I couldn't decide what to do.
Unable to see, I heard my name being called.
Then I walked outside.

—RUMI

Questions for Reflection

1. What ideas come to your mind when hear "Relatedness?"

2. What are some memories of moments in which you felt special relatedness?

3. How does relatedness support you in your walk and your work?

4. As a leader, what would you like to draw on more in your relatedness?

5. At this moment, where are you taking a step of growth in your power of relatedness?

Vulnerability and Compassion
Working in Circles
Conversation
Gathering Wisdom

Vulnerability and Compassion

A question my mother frequently asked when she didn't like something I did was, "Just exactly *who* do you think you are?" My usual, shamefaced response was, "Nobody." Nobody; not even an authentic "somebody." Today, however, my answer might be "Everybody," as I gain understanding of our underlying connection through our humanity. You and I are connected to each other whether we ever meet or not. We live together in human community and are interdependent with the larger community of life.

Within the workplace, we often let ourselves and each other down by losing myriad opportunities for connecting with each other and missing out on the resulting potential for human fulfillment. Sometimes at work, disclosing feelings, concerns, and dreams is viewed, at best, as weakness—and at worst as revealing information that can later be used against you. At other times, dropping everything to be present and fully listen to another who is vulnerable is seen as inappropriate or inefficient. Where such assumptions rule, settings tend to be sterile and devoid of the wholeness of our lives, devoid of what *really* matters. People can work side by side and be unaware of the most important things occurring in each other's lives—a dying parent, a child failing at school, a miscarriage, a marriage in chaos. A friend of mine, while going through the greatest trauma of her life—having been diagnosed with cancer—didn't want anyone at work to know. How have we created and enabled such isolating environments in the place where many of us spend the majority of our waking hours? More important, what can we do to change them?

Vulnerability and compassion are interactive and involve giving and receiving simultaneously. Intimacy is allowing others to see into you and seeing into them as well; as my friend Michele calls it, "into-me-see." When you are vulnerable and disclose your truth and inner life, you allow others to have a window onto your soul. With that window comes the possibility for becoming connected. Of course you risk being hurt, abandoned, laughed at or in some other way judged. It goes with the territory. Yet, the richness of closeness and acceptance, when it occurs, can be so satisfying and magical that the desire for connection overtakes and dissipates the losses or fears.

Compassion is being fully present, really listening to, and being with, another. Through such presence you are given the possibility of clearly seeing into the soul of another. Here, the other person takes the vulnerable risks while you, in your compassion, must manage your fears, your judgments, and your tendencies toward jumping in to "fix" the other person.

At the deep levels of your humanness, you have universal underlying concerns, needs, and experiences. Vulnerability and compassion establish common ground between you and everyone else. Through experiences eliciting your vulnerability and your compassion, you learn that you are not alone. Others' disclosures offer you an opportunity to develop and express empathy and compassion. Listening brings the possibility of validity and release to both your own life and to the lives of others.

Working in Circles

Depending on a group's purpose, differing amounts of intimacy, from almost none to a great deal, may be necessary. Determining what each situation requires is critical. For example, a team working to reduce errors through new work processes requires less exchange of compassion and vulnerability than does a diversity task force where longheld painful individual experiences surface in the workplace .

The circle is ancient and common in human interaction and relatedness. From stories of the hunt around the nighttime fire to quilting bees, from children's games to square dancing, from book clubs to support groups, the circle is a primary organizing structure. In modern business, however, the triangle has been a more familiar organizing structure than the circle, at least until recently.

A recent, high-profile template in business organizations is "self-directed teams." If not clearly defined, however, "self-directed" can leave people new to working in circles with dashed expectations, because they tend to equate self-directed with "unmanaged" or "autonomous." It may appear to an outside observer that a team is operating autonomously; but to be truly effective, team structures, no matter what they are called, require *more* organizational interdependence and integration than do top-down organizations. Each team or circle is a component of a larger system of interlocking circles. To use an analogy, a self-directed eye or leg is a problem for your entire body. Your eyes and legs have independent tasks and unique functions, but they serve a larger whole. In fact, that's *all* they do. They are part of the hierarchical system of your body.

As circles are being introduced into organizations there is often a tendency toward "either/or" thinking; many members of the organization conclude that forming teams means eliminating the hierarchy. Rather than *either* hierarchy *or* teams, the focus needs to be on finding the most productive interaction between the two forms. The merging of the triangle and circle in organizational structure is an evolutionary leap for Western culture. Hierarchy has been the primary organizing principle for getting work done in the West at least since the Roman Legions. Teams have been present throughout human history—primarily outside the Western workplace. Blending hierarchy and team is a deep and powerful change for business organizations. While there are templates about what teamwork is and how teams "should" look, the most successful teams find their own way by tapping into the energy already present within their circles.

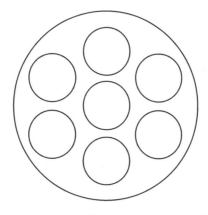

Myth of Self-Directed Teams

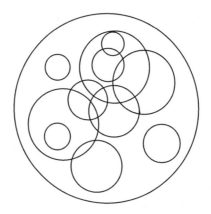

Reality of Self-Directed Teams

Teams develop best when they are based on clear communal goals, the existing passions and interests of team members, and a candid understanding of their members' dissatisfactions and desires for change.

Teams are webs of relationships. Relationships are intricate networks in which everything is connected to everything else. No matter where you begin, you will touch all aspects. Thus circles are in continuous motion. Progress occurs by moving through iterations, each approximation coming closer to your ideal.

Along with communal *task* goals, circles also need clear communal *process* agreements and goals. Process goals are reminders that it is the journey itself, and the inns along the way, that offer meaning. In human journeys, perfect or final destinations are elusive illusions. You and everyone you know is headed toward an unique individual destination; for particular periods of time, you travel a road together as a team. Building work teams is a dynamic, ever-changing, ever-evolving expression of human interaction. Attempts to "achieve" or solidify them in time, space, membership, or other physical attributes can cause their tender, vulnerable, ever-shifting nature to crumble or shatter.

Conversation

One of the most powerful possibilities circles share is the ability to challenge assumptions collectively through engaging in dialogue or deep, open conversation. Of course, deep, open conversation is not new. What *is* new is having ongoing forums for it at work.

An information-systems department of more than one hundred people, attempting to mirror organically the work they do, had organized themselves into a network of self-directed teams. Because the managers didn't want to interfere with the teams' development, they had distanced themselves. They did so with the best intentions, but before the teams were ready; in consequence, many of the teams felt abandoned. People recognized a need to learn more of what was required of them and how they could best work together. We set up an ongoing conversation between employees and managers. Our first agreement was to meet three times, and then evaluate. Some, especially some managers, thought that sitting in a room together for a half-day a month would be wasted time with no concrete output. Nonetheless, everyone agreed to experiment, to give it a try. We explored tools to help form the boundaries of a "container" and to establish purpose. Specifically, for example, we used Angeles

Arrien's principles of *The Fourfold Way* to establish ground rules for dialogue. They are:

- Show up.
- Pay attention to what has heart and meaning.
- Speak the truth without blame or judgment.
- Be open rather than attached to outcome.

The purpose of the dialogue was twofold: to genuinely hear and seek to understand each other through the outer conversation, and for each person to explore personal assumptions through "listening" to the conversation inside his or her head. We used "The Ladder of Inference" from *The Learning Organization Field Guide* as a way to describe to the power of that inner conversation.

A fun and funny conversation occurred in response to an employee's question about how the managers decided who got the "plum" assignments. More importantly, however, it revealed assumptions that the group was able to alter from that point forward.

The employees' view was, "You sit together behind closed doors, smoking cigars and developing your long-range 'battle plan.' That plan predetermines the fate of our careers, but we just don't know what it is yet." When they heard that, the managers' mouths fell open. One said, "I wish we were so organized! We have no idea who's going to be doing what. We don't even know what the 'plum' assignments are or when they'll show up. Usually what happens is that we find out on a Tuesday that we need someone in Japan by Friday. We get out the list and look at who's got the skill, who can leave what they're doing, whose family can handle the separation..." The "pure" rules of dialogue fell by the way—with nothing of significance lost in that enlightening moment where underlying assumption on the part of the managers surfaced—as one employee interjected, "Hold on! You mean you decide based on what you know about our family

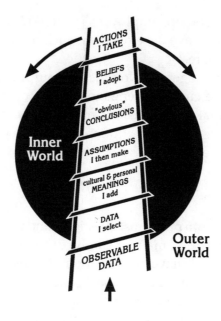

Ladder of Inference

situations?" "Well, yes, it seems like the kind and fair thing to do," another manager responded.

What followed was a conversation of how what the managers thought was "kind and fair" the employees found patronizing and controlling. The outcome was that the managers, with some feelings of relief, agreed to learn from employees what they considered plum assignments and, whenever possible, to include more employees in future decision-making about staff assignments.

As mentioned, the members of this conversation had agreed to experiment for three sessions. During the third session we looked at whether anything of value had happened. All wanted to continue. Especially rewarding was listening to the managers who had assumed it would be a waste of time. As one commented, "So much has occurred in these conversations. I've learned a lot about how employees see things." Another raised the question,

"How can we get more employees involved?" and followed it with, "I feel like I have developed so much more trust with each of you. I want more."

No preplanned agenda. No specified output required. Just a chance to sit in a circle and engage in deep, open conversation about how to make relationships function optimally, make the workplace more satisfying, and make both the present and the future a mutual endeavor.

Gathering Wisdom

Looking deeply into problems, questions, and proposals for decisions in a disciplined manner can be difficult and taxing. For starters, individuals have personal opinions and judgments that differ. Sometimes personalities clash, and some people are more skilled than others at getting heard and influencing. What follows is one possibility for how you can ensure getting the best input possible, whether you are leading a group or participating as a member.

This possibility is the Native American council process taught by WindEagle and RainbowHawk, teachers of the EHAMA Institute of Los Gatos, CA. There are eight perspectives, based on the eight directions of a circle called The Medicine Wheel. A final filter, consisting of two core principles called The Two Sacred Laws, comprise The Children's Fire at the center. (These core principles are described in Chapter 6, "Bridge People.") The council process can be used to gather wisdom and information on challenging issues and to make consensus decisions that best serve everyone.

Consensus is not necessarily about agreement.

My initial desire was to write about The Way of the Council by describing the content of the teaching as I had received it. But I had an uneasiness about what I was presenting and how I was presenting it. My experience had been so rich; but when the model was down on paper, it seemed so one dimensional. I asked WindEagle and RainbowHawk to review the draft. Through their response I better understood my discomfort. They wrote back, "Our suggestion [is] to…not try to present the teaching itself but to speak of what it illuminated or stimulated or made clear in some way…. The reason we would not choose to present the teaching itself is that the experience of being there is so important to the learning and the integration. We would want to encourage people to seek the experience rather than read it."

One illumination of my experience with the council process is that it has redefined "consensus" to being more than (at best) getting agreement and, if not agreement, at least having everyone agree that they can live with the outcome. In fact, I learned that consensus is not necessarily about agreement at all. For consensus to work, there must be agreement that an outcome of no consensus is acceptable. Considerable difference can emerge when a group sits in council. Collective wisdom can only fully come forth when there is allowance for differences and disagreement. Quoted in Peter Carlin's article "How to Make a Decision Like a Tribe," WindEagle notes, "If there's agreement, that's good. If there's disagreement, at least we've heard it in depth and we can establish what it is. This process is not about positions, it's about people… It creates relationship, connection, and respect. When you speak and you're different from me, I value your opinion. If we can live that way, we'll be wiser in the actions we take."

The Board of Directors of the World Business Academy used The Way of the Council during our annual board retreat. We created a sacred circle by coming together with commitment, sincerity, and respect for each other and for our process. As we sat together, I witnessed myself dropping judgments based on my past experiences with people. Instead I saw and heard the wise, genuine, and heartfelt convictions of each person. As the wisdom was gathered around the circle, to my surprise, I became less and less attached to my personal points of view and experienced a growing openness to trusting the collective. For me, the council process served as a medium to foster group trust and integrity.

For the council process to work well, each of us sitting together agreed to participate in very specific ways and to adhere to a particular structure. We each agreed to:

- Represent one of the eight perspectives.
- Represent the assigned or chosen perspective for *all* involved, whether directly or indirectly. In our case, this included such stakeholders, as members, staff, potential members, and families.
- Trust the holders of the various perspectives to bring forth the wisdom of that perspective wholly and with integrity, no matter what our personal biases may be.
- Listen deeply to what has heart and meaning as it is offered from each of the perspectives.
- Honor the "collective mind" as it unfolds, and uphold the outcome achieved as a collective.

As RainbowHawk says in "How to Make a Decision Like a Tribe," "When the council comes together, it's a cumulative process, rather than a debating process. Being…in the council means stepping forward for the whole. Each person adds to it and as each adds, the container of wisdom gets fuller."

One of three outcomes occurs after hearing all of the wisdom available:

- Consensus becomes self-evident, not through personal opinion or individual influence but rather through aggregated wisdom culminating by passing the filter of the core principles. A step can be taken on a question; *a decision can be made* on a proposal.
- It becomes evident that there is insufficient information or wisdom to reach consensus. It *remains an open item* and the group may agree to gather whatever additional data is necessary.

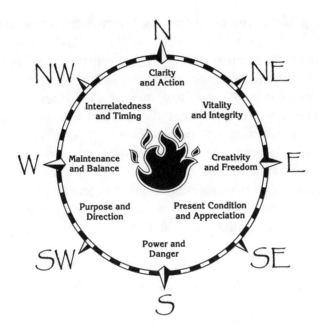

The Eight Council Perspectives

- The question or proposal does not pass the test of upholding The Two Sacred Laws of The Children's Fire at the center of the circle. *It is "dead"* as a direction or decision.

Such a process takes time and guidance to learn and practice. So does any new learning or skill development. Yet, as a group becomes more facile, the amount of time needed diminishes in most cases. Within a context—such as a work setting—all questions and proposals are connected to one another. You can apply wisdom to a new issue by updating and adding to what you have gathered for previous issues. In other words, after some time of working together, it is possible for your group to gather wisdom informally or "on the fly"—in hallways, at lunch, at the copy machine.

George McCown of McCown De Lueew, who serves as Chairman of the Board of Directors of the World Business Academy, introduced the council process to his venture banking group. Holding council, he found, offers a way for the partners to be heard, for all sides of issues to come forth, for differences to surface. "When we're up against a really tough issue, we go into council," says McCown as he enthusiastically describes "sitting" in council. "It's one of those rare things you encounter in life that people immediately 'get.' It resonates at a very deep level. And it gives you permission not only to 'get off' your position but also to sit in someone else's position. When a group is willing to trust the council process, it can have extraordinary, highly creative outcomes."

Formally sitting together in council is a way to learn, to leverage differences as assets, to approach and achieve consensus, to make decisions backed with commitment, and to increase trust between members of a group. Through it, you have an opportunity to experience new levels of possibility; experience new relatedness; surface limiting beliefs; and increase the levels of integrity, balance, and creativity of your decisions both individually and as organizations.

Vulnerability and compassion, conversation, and sitting in council are examples of primary ingredients for developing a connected circle. They help you to find common ground. When this connection occurs, you recognize it in the same way you recognize, for example, that individual beads only make a necklace because of a string linking them. The beads are the necklace you see, but only because the string provides an invisible connection between the beads. It is such a connection that goes deep inside to the level of our souls. Group processes that have high integrity result in tangible, concrete output; but they also have the seemingly intangible, invisible output of rewarding human kinship and relatedness.

Chapter 12

The Power of Expression

...Start doing things you think should be done, and start being what you think society should become. Do you believe in free speech? Then speak freely. Do you love the truth? Then tell it. Do you believe in an open society? Then act in the open. Do you believe in a decent and humane society? Then behave decently and humanely.

—ADAM MICHNIK, AN ARCHITECT OF POLAND'S SOLIDARITY MOVEMENT

Questions for Reflection

1. What ideas come to your mind when you hear "Expression?"

2. What are some memories of times you felt especially expressive?

3. How does expression support you in your walk and your work?

4. As a leader, how would you like to draw on more expression?

5. At this moment, where are you taking a step of growth in your power of expression?

Speaking Personal Truth
Generative Learning
Manifestation

Speaking Personal Truth

Many messages in organizations suggest that you inhibit yourself from speaking the truth as you see it. Why are there such limitations? Why agree to them?

In *A Wizard of Earthsea,* the first book of her "Earthsea Trilogy," Ursula LeGuin writes of a young boy who is studying to become a wizard. One portion of his apprenticeship journey is to live with and learn from different master wizards. One wizard is The Namer; from him the boy learns to speak, with reverence and wisdom, the "real" names of everything. The wizard teaches him that naming has enormous power for when we speak the real name of something it no longer has power over us. Naming diffuses fear.

As mentioned earlier, one of my own fears is that of being seen as a fool. This book is a business book and yet it contains little that is objective or rational. Thus, now and then I fear the judgments of stereotypical "real" business people. Then one day, as I was struggling to write honestly in the midst of my fear, I broke open a fortune cookie and read: "Wise men learn much from fools!" "Yes," I thought to myself, "even if perceived a fool, I can speak what is true for me."

Fear of being punished or rejected at best submerges enormous potential for creativity and connection; at worst, fear extinguishes such potential altogether. One way to control others within the workplace is to judge them incompetent, ignorant fools. It only works, however, if the people being judged agree to self-regulate, self-limit, and comply.

Tremendous creative energy can go into hiding the truth.

To find out where you self-regulate, self-limit, or comply, you can explore what payoffs (most likely negative) you are receiving when not speaking your truth brings you pain and unhappiness. One "payoff" might be the close connection you make with others who experience similar pain. This kind of connection, however, is based on what is *not* working, rather than on what is. Tremendous creative energy can go into hiding the truth, or hiding from the truth; walking on eggshells; worrying about what *might* happen, and then being angry when nothing changes. Yet, those you deem the source of your pain are unlikely to change if they are unaware of their impact.

Imagine that you have a series of silent, invisible hoops in front of you. These hoops represent your values, ethics, and the things you want and expect in a relationship. In general, in our work cultures, we tend not to tell others what these hoops are. Those who manage to jump through become friends or trusted colleagues. Those who fail to jump through end up rejected or as adversaries. Working with someone who hasn't made it through your hoops often results in a strained or volatile relationship. Yet, if you can articulate the hoops that have been missed as soon as you are able to identify them, you have more options for the relationship than the either/or of friend and foe.

I was in conflict with others in a group of which I am a member. I became angry when behavior continued that I didn't like, especially with the person in the leadership position. Yet I avoided telling him directly, because I feared his blustery style. I complained to a friend, also a member, who empathized with me. She did the same with me. We became very close in our unhappiness and frustration. Now and then one or the other of us would make a foray into the eye of what we considered the storm, but never for long. At last a time came when I had an opportunity to say everything fully and clearly. To my shock and surprise, the leader apologized for his part. As time passed,

I experienced positive changes in my relationship with him. Meantime, my confidante also has done her direct communication toward completion. As a result, she and I have had to find other bases for our relationship. Today our connection is less intense but more luxurious.

Remember the Rolaids commercials? They were about seeking temporary relief; *connecting against* rather than speaking directly is seeking temporary relief. Connecting against helps you feel less isolated. It feels good for a while, but the problem inevitably returns. Under the surface, even when connecting against, you continue to have the anger, fear, or anxiousness that lead to feelings of isolation. Rolaids do not deal with cause. They simply appease the symptoms. So it is with connecting against.

Rather than relying on temporary relief, seek a healthy diet instead. In other words, look for and treat the cause of the problem, rather than merely the symptoms. The healthy-diet cycle may begin in the same way as the temporary relief cycle: with a feeling of isolation because of something that has happened. But the next step is *connecting directly with* whomever is involved. The result is an opportunity to complete the feelings and move on. Completion or resolution may not always be what you want or expect, however. You do not have the right to control another with your personal truth. You merely have the right to speak it. But, no matter what the outcome, the "air" is clearer and cleaner. There is possibility for direct connection. If not with the others involved, at a minimum you can experience a renewed connection within yourself for having taken a stand by speaking your truth.

When you truly listen, you glimpse the heart and soul of another.

It is beneficial to be able to speak in ways that others can hear. Your truth allows others to see into your heart; it opens a window onto your soul. The reverse is also true, of course. When you truly listen, you glimpse the heart and soul of another. No matter how bumpy and awkward, the interaction of speaking directly and listening deeply is critical for connection.

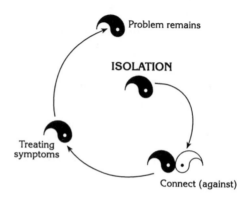

Rolaids

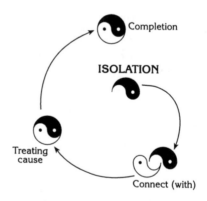

Healthy Diet

When you make mistakes—like blaming when trying to speak directly, or defending yourself rather than listening—skills for recovering become essential. You might want to take a break, regroup, and breathe before beginning again. Then, the primary skill remains the same: to continue to speak your truth and listen to the other's truth in turn. Feeling sad about being angry? Say it. Feeling embarrassed about your clumsiness? Say it. Wanting forgiveness? Say it. Recovery from mistakes, discomforts, or disagreements is more important than doing it "right," more important than being correct, more important than thinking alike.

Seeking to recover is not always required. However, it is required where you want to demonstrate your investment in the relationship; your caring and trust in the other person; your confidence that, together, you are smart enough to figure out how to move forward.

Speaking the truth serves as an efficient filter. It draws in kindred spirits. We recognize truth in each other just like we recognize integrity. Truth is an expression of integrity. Kindred spirits may agree or have wildly different values and opinions. Their connection is in authenticity and personal truth.

Generative Learning

Peter Senge's book *The Fifth Discipline* is about creating "learning organizations." A distinction is made between "adaptive" and "generative" learning. Adaptive learning is based on survival. Generative learning creates the future. Generative learning is both the *motivation for* and the *result of* individual and group creativity. In order to engage creatively, you first must identify commonly held assumptions of your workplace. Then you must investigate to see which ones are limiting your ability to learn generatively.

An example of an assumption that limits us globally is the recently popularized word "sustainability." "Sustain" is not a word of hope or creation. It means "maintain," "shore up," "buttress." An alternative word that is more generative is "viability." Viable means "alive," "vital," "prospering." Sustainability does little to engender deep images of thriving. It stops at notions of surviving because it implicitly calls for adaptive or survival learning, rather than generative or creative learning.

As with speaking the truth, as with taking a stand, there are risks to engaging boldly in generative learning. Sometimes, for example, it results in seeing the garden in a whole new way. It results in creating new forces, new forms, new systems, and new ceremonies. Moreover, with the new can come chaos—at least for a time.

You are created to learn and create. All you do is learn and create—one thing or another, helpful or unhelpful, pleasing or displeasing. It is the nature of human design. Through your thoughts, your desires, your passions, and your connectedness with others, you learn and create. Therefore, it is critical to think through consciously what you *want* to create, as well as why and how you want to create it. What do you *intend* to create? Become clear and your clarity can serve as a beacon for your creativity, giving it focus, range, and radiance.

Manifestation

In the movie *Apollo 13*, after a party to watch Neil Armstrong walking on the moon, the character of Jim Lovell says to his wife, "We now live in a world where man has walked on the moon. It's not a miracle. We just decided to go."

Ideas become "real" when we manifest them in the physical world. Every tangible result of human creativity was a dream or idea first: Stone Age tools and computers; gardens and gourmet food; strategic plans and new products; children and works of art. Each is the result of human creativity.

While consulting within a Fortune 100 company, I had an opportunity to visit with the CEO. Answering his query, I related my vision for a more viable world. After some time he asked, "Tell me, do you expect to finish this task in your lifetime?" The question left me breathless; *finishing* had never entered my mind! Yet, it also helped me more deeply understand his work and his focus on physically manifesting; on leaving a concrete, completed legacy behind.

Those of you who have built homes have seen your dreams take physical form. You have watched a dream, which you may even have thought at some point to be an impossible dream, become an idea. The idea then became drawings and plans that, in turn, "developed" into raw materials. The raw materials, when integrated, became a completed structure. Finally these integrated raw materials, called a "house," became a home when you infused yourself. Perhaps you built a fire in the fireplace, put music into the air, played with your children in the yard, cooked with your favorite spices and produced delicious aromas on the stove, appreciated vistas beyond the windows. However your home became physically real, it began as an idea in your mind.

Speaking personal truth and demonstrating creative action through learning and manifesting are primary means of offering your unique talents and skills to the world.

Chapter 13

The Power of Perspective

Mommy, why do I have to be little before I can be big?

—Michael Abelardo Shipka

I've often thought there ought to be a manual to hand to little kids, telling them what kind of planet they're on, why they don't fall off it, how much time they've probably got here, how to avoid poison ivy... I tried to write one once. It was called Welcome to Earth. But I got stuck on explaining why we don't fall off the planet.

—Kurt Vonnegut, Jr.

Questions for Reflection

1. What ideas come to your mind when you hear "Perspective?"

2. What are some memories of times you felt you had perspective?

3. How does perspective support you in your walk and your work?

4. As a leader, how would you like to draw more on perspective?

5. At this moment, where are you taking a step of growth in your power of perspective?

Enlarging the Context
Cultivating a Field of View
Thinking Holistically

Enlarging the Context

It was mid-afternoon, the sun was relentless, and we had spent hours walking in the splendor of the temples of Luxor. "It's so hot and I'm tired," Aida said. "Let's ride back to our hotel." So the three of us, all teachers at the same school in Beirut, hired a horse-drawn buggy. As we made our way south along the river, the Egyptian driver and my friends, all native Arabic speakers, carried on a conversation. Though I usually liked participating with my basic Arabic, on this occasion I let my mind wander elsewhere.

Later, with much delight, Aida and Shaheen reported what had transpired. "The driver wanted to know how wide the Nile was where you come from, Barbara," Aida said. "Shaheen told him that the Nile didn't flow there. He was amazed to hear that and had a hard time believing it. Then he asked her, 'But how can people *live* without the Nile?'"

After contemplating it for a few days, we concluded that perhaps his question wasn't so funny after all. Any direction in which he traveled related him to the Nile; he might go into lifeless desert, or lush, green settlements like his own. His entire world either lived by the Nile, or died without it.

Many people from all over the world excitedly visit Luxor. Most visitors don't speak Arabic. So our driver's exposure to a larger world remained limited. In fact, with so many people visiting Luxor, he could reasonably conclude that he lived at the very center of the universe. After all, people from all over the world came to where *he* was.

He isn't alone in holding this view. The orientation of being at the center of what matters has little to do with language, education, or income level. Even though you and I have much more experience than did that driver with maps and time zones, distances and cultures, we too operate as though wherever we are is the center. We maintain that notion until we consciously shift our attention in order to consider a larger reality.

The center of the universe extends far beyond your individual street address and the routes upon which you travel in your daily routines. To develop a holistic perspective you must consciously choose to see more than individual events, to hear more than the literal level of words spoken.

When you enlarge your context, you listen for *essence and meaning*, for what is behind and beneath the literal words spoken. In asking "How wide is the Nile where she lives?" the buggy driver was really asking, "What is the source-of-water-that-maintains-life where she comes from?"

Cultivating a Field of View

When you focus on a point of view, things often seem more complex, overwhelming, and harder to solve than they need to be. Developing a larger "field of view" can make holding paradox and working with and within complexity much easier.

The Six-Day and Yom Kippur Wars marked the edges of my time in Lebanon, though the conflict they were part of was ongoing all the while I lived there. Aida, a Palestinian, had very strong political views; because we were friends, I adopted some of them. Once, she invited me to spend a weekend with her and other friends in the village of her birth. It was in the south, along what was then the Israeli border. I obtained special permission from the government as it was a restricted area; we passed through several military checkpoints along the way. We arrived late at night under a multitude of stars and no moon; rolling hills silhouetted by olive trees marking the black horizon. I imagined myself in a serene biblical night scene not much different from what Jesus might have experienced.

Except for one thing: electricity. Salah, Aida's brother, pointed to the many villages that dotted the landscape and asked, "Do you see how the lights are yellow in some villages and white in others? The yellow," he continued, "is incandescent lighting in Arab villages—both in Lebanon and across the border in Israel—and the white is florescent lighting in new Israeli settlements." They appeared to be peacefully intermingled. But the next morning, my illusion of serenity and peacefulness was shattered. What had been hidden by the blanket of darkness were the tanks, trenches, barbed wire, and soldiers in formation all across the horizon near the crest of the hills.

A few years later I journeyed to Israel and stayed with a family on a *moshav*, or collective farm, in the Golan Heights near the Lebanese border. Eva, my hostess, and her cousin, Yuri, were the only members of their German family to survive the horrors of World War II. She had emigrated to Israel and he to England, where he flew back and forth to Israel for El Al Airlines. People in this region carried machine guns as a daily routine. Nearly every family in Israel had lost someone to the ongoing conflict, culminating most recently with the Yom Kippur War. Listening to Eva's stories and her sincere wishes for peace and reconciliation, I found myself opening to hear this "other side." I told Eva about my visit to Aida's village; she offered to take me to see the same vista, but from an Israeli perspective. Thus, I looked back over the trenches, tanks, barbed wire and soldiers at the Lebanese village where I had been. My mind wrestled with how to reconcile these two opposing, equally genuine "points of view."

I noticed I no longer had an opinion about who was "right" and who was "wrong" in this complex situation. I learned that having no opinion can result just as easily from having too much information as from lacking information. With first-hand information on a human scale from both sides of the conflict, I developed greater recognition of the complexity. Having literally stood on both sides of the conflict, I saw more than a point of view. The range of my sight was developing into a "field of view."

In many cases, a point of view narrows potential. Your point of view, composed of your interpretations, makes a huge difference in what is or is not possible. If the point from which you view is limited, your possibilities are also limited. A field of view does not replace your point of view but rather augments and gives context to it. Points of view tend toward "either/or" orientations. A field of view allows you potential for turning either/or into both/and.

For example, in exploring what is changing in business, many graphs and charts have appeared to describe the "new paradigm." Typically, they lay out contrasting aspects of the old and new paradigms in two columns. The left-hand column describes predominantly the dark side of the "old," and the right-hand column describes predominantly the bright side of the "new." These descriptions are useful in helping us envision what we would like to shed, as well as possibilities within our grasp. Qualities that are often mentioned in these comparisons include:

Old	New
Mechanistic	Organic
Direct and control	Shared responsibility
Hierarchy	Teams
Image	Authenticity
Power over others	Power with others
Permanence	Fluidity

These distinctions are helpful—but two cautions are necessary. First, there is much about the "old" that is of value to retain for the future, and that can provide stability in the present. Secondly, in enthusiasm and desire, many attempts are made to leap from the left-hand column straight across to the right-hand column. The results are often disappointment ("We tried teams, and they didn't work"), frustration ("We decided to share the responsibility, and people aren't keeping their bargains"), fear ("I'm not showing my real feelings after what happened"), and feelings of failure ("I know everyone wanted it to work. Where d̄ ɟ we go wrong?"). It's important to keep in mind that the right-hand column represents a *vision* of a final destination. Getting from where we are to the vision of where we want to be can only be done by means of a series of approximations.

Thus, neither the left nor the right column is where "the action" is. The action is in the empty white space *between* the two columns. Yet this critically important region is virtually unseen. That empty white space is not a void; rather, it is pregnant with life and movement. Quantum leaps in evolution and instantaneous miracles of change do occur. However, most often in day-to-day life, you cannot leap over the white space from the left and successfully arrive on the right. In one way or another, through trial and error, experimentation, and research and development you must walk to get from here to there, from your current state to our ideal.

Thinking Holistically

Thinking holistically or systemically develops your field of view. Holistic thinking is more than strategic thinking, though that is part of it. In thinking systemically you maintain an awareness of how any action you take "over here" affects everything else, here, there, and into the future. Whenever pressure is applied to change one part of a system, it has an impact on other parts of that system—sometimes in totally unintended ways. For example, during the Gulf War an embargo was placed on Iraq. While it was intended to place hardship on Saddam Hussein and his government, we can now see other parts of the system that were negatively impacted. Within Iraq, Iraqi women and children suffered. Beyond Iraq, Sri Lankans suffered; Iraq was one of the world's biggest customers for Sri Lankan tea.

Whether you hold a precise point of view or a broader field of view, you have influence through the decisions you make. Some of your decisions have impact far beyond what you imagined, sometimes in very different parts of the system than you might have expected or considered. Continuously enlarging your picture, your sense of context, and your comprehension of complexity increases your understanding of the impact of your decisions.

When thinking holistically you can grasp and hold whole, complex, often apparently paradoxical pictures and thoughts in your mind. You seek the interrelatedness of everything—both within and beyond a particular issue, person, business, event, or problem. Think again of the *Tai Ji* symbol of yin and yang with its interrelatedness of light and dark and the dynamic dots of the opposite sides. The whole encompasses both my seventh-story dream with its apparently dark apocalyptic message and the light-filled, glorious achievements of space travel.

When thinking systemically you can resist treating only symptoms while delving more deeply to ascertain cause. For example, consider our growing practice of recycling. Many of us have become more "responsible" through becoming recyclers, developing a routine of separating our bottles from cans, our paper from our cardboard. As we haul our recycling bins to the curb we are lulled into a sense of complacency, because we are treating symptoms over cause. The cause is "upriver." When we truly take responsibility for cause over symptom in this case, we will demand finding ways to avoid creating waste in the first place.

Health care provides another opportunity to observe the difference between cause and symptom. In the predominant paradigm of Western medicine, the absence of any apparent symptom is synonymous with good health. We are taught to go to doctors for periodic check-ups. Other than that, most of us go to the doctor only when we have symptoms. Western medicine is superb at diagnosing disease and treating catastrophic illness and accidents. However, it does not teach us much about how to be well and maintain our own wellness.

Some of us are gaining a systemic view of health as holistic and traditional indigenous medical approaches and practices enter our lives and augment the strengths of Western medicine. As one example, Earl Bakken, a co-founder of Medtronic—a corporation well known for its cardiac pacemakers—is involved with establishing a hospital in Hawaii that, under one roof, offers services ranging from a native kahuna healer to the highest of the high-tech equipment.

Holistic medicine serves as a touchstone from which we can extrapolate what it means to be whole and healthy in all areas of our lives, work, and thinking. Some basic premises are:

- Personal responsibility and ability to be well.
- Partnership in prevention.
- Seeking cause over symptom.
- Working in harmony with nature.

In "Seeing the Garden in a Whole New Way," I spoke of changes in smoking habits as an example of interactive systems change. There's more to the story. I attended stop-smoking classes at a local hospital. I chewed Nicoban. I threw packs of cigarettes out the car window on my way home after the classes—only to stop at the next gas station to buy yet another pack of Marlboros.

I had heard that acupuncture worked for some people so I visited a holistic health clinic near my home. After two treatments I felt euphoric and stopped smoking—for four days. I canceled the third treatment because of the shame I felt. Finally, I mustered my courage and returned. The doctor responded compassionately. "Let's set aside the acupuncture treatments for a while," he suggested. "Imagine a swimming pool, full to the top. You're the pool, and your stress level is the water. Imagine throwing a huge boulder into that pool. That's quitting smoking for you. Since the pool is full and the boulder huge, a lot of water will be thrown out of the pool. Let's take three months to work together on lowering the water level of your swimming pool before we throw any more boulders in. Okay?" Though I didn't know what he specifically meant, I got the picture and agreed.

Lowering the water level included my first experiences with structural chiropractic treatments; a complete change in diet; weekly sessions with a coach to learn how to breathe; and writing in a journal as a way of learning, and learning to change my negative and limiting beliefs. Lowering the water level was, thus, a combination of "therapies" that tended my physical, emotional, mental, and spiritual needs.

On a pre-determined date three months later I went back to once again begin a series of four acupuncture treatments. I still remember the date and what I was wearing. But I don't remember actually smoking my last cigarette. I never craved another cigarette after that day; I didn't even have the three other treatments. Was it a miracle? Maybe; but I think it was my readiness to attend to the whole of my being. Rather than treating only symptoms, my doctor helped me change my mind and treat myself—my self. Together, we saw me as a whole, self-regulating system.

His suggestions were "high leverage" points for change— where relatively small amounts of intervention, mixed with large amounts of tenacity, held the potential of resulting in enormous changes in my whole system. The same principles that apply to people as a whole systems apply to organizations as whole systems. Just as you or I can be treated as whole beings with myriad forms of high-leverage, self-regulating abilities to change, so can *any* system—no matter what size or configuration. Profound changes can occur in organizations when we attend to organization wellness and wholeness, seek cause over symptom, see organizations as natural systems, and look to prevent fires rather than fight them.

Dee Hock, CEO emeritus of VISA USA and VISA International, built that organization using principles he calls "chaordic." He defines a chaord as "any self-organizing, adaptive, nonlinear, complex system, whether physical, biological, or social, the behavior of which exhibits characteristics of both order and chaos..." 23,000 financial institutions create VISA's product. VISA cards are used in scores of countries by 355 million people; in fact, they have come to constitute the largest block of consumer purchasing power in the world. Yet, Hock writes, "In the legal sense, VISA is a non-stock, for-profit, membership corporation. In another sense, it is *an inside-out holding company* in that it does not hold but is held by its functioning parts." The 23,000 financial institutions are, all at the same time, VISA's owners, members, and customers. VISA lives or dies by natural, organic, holistic principles.

The principles of perspective—enlarging the context, developing a field of view, and holistic thinking—apply to all levels: the individual, work groups, organizations, or the entire economic system. Perspective allows us to hold a big picture and grasp both focus and field, both symptom and cause, both old and new and the path connecting them.

Chapter 14

The Power of Reverence

Sitting in front of his master, the student posed the question, "All the mountains, rivers, lakes, the earth, the sun, the moon and the stars, where do they come from?" In answer, the master replied, "Where does your question come from?"

—Zen story

Questions for Reflection

1. What ideas come to your mind when you hear "Reverence?"

2. What are some memories of times you felt especially reverent?

3. How does reverence support you in your walk and your work?

4. As a leader, how would you like to draw more on reverence?

5. At this moment, where are you taking a step of growth in your power of reverence?

Grace and Humility
Service and Elderwork
Honoring Mystery

Grace and Humility

Engaging in the fullness of life, with wisdom and awareness, results in an experience of grace. Grace is remembering, in the moment, that you are alive. You breathe in and you breathe out; grace is noticing that you have been breathing in and out without noticing it. What a miracle! Simply breathing in and out is more miraculous than landing on the moon.

Grace is remembering, in the moment, that you are alive.

Recently I had an opportunity to see my own live blood on video. An especially poignant moment came when I saw a white blood cell moving to engulf bacteria. I watched, breathlessly comprehending the drama occurring in my body. I cannot feel, see, hear, taste, or smell it, but it happens anyway. The design of life is a design of grace. It is a mystery in its rarest and most mystical sense because it may always defy our desire for comprehension; it may always remain mysterious.

You experience grace on the mornings you wake up realizing you have another day to be in your life, receiving both its gifts and challenges. And beyond what is occurring within your body to maintain your life without your conscious awareness, you also can consciously create your life once again, day by day, more and more to your liking. Grace is surrender into the goodness and perfection of life. You may still experience anxiety about the future, regret about the past, or fear of loss of what you have in the present. Nonetheless, there is perfection in simply being alive. Whether healthy or ill, you are safe and supported, just as you are.

Humility allows you to join the human condition rather than be above it.

Noticing grace—both the mystery and the perfection—results in feeling truly humble. Though they may be easily confused, humility and submission have little or nothing in common. Submission is demonstrated through being self-effacing or having low self-esteem. In contrast, humility increases rather than diminishes you. It is a recognition of the mystery that is God—or whatever name you use to describe unknown, awesome patterns and creative forces in the universe; it is a connection to the source of all life beyond and within you. And, most specifically, humility connects you to your humanity. It allows you to join the human condition rather than be above it. It reinforces the truth that you are one miraculous part of the mystery that is life and compels you to honor and seek harmony with all life no matter what its form.

Service and Elderwork

For ten years I had taught in elementary schools around the world, trained Peace Corps volunteers, and worked for non-profit organizations. Entering my first job in the corporate world, I felt intimidated. I thought people in business were smarter than people in education and non-profit groups; certainly they were more "successful." I was still measuring success as accumulated power and monetary wealth. I quickly learned that many people in business are not necessarily smarter than anyone else—and even those who are smarter are not necessarily wiser. It takes great intelligence to build a high-producing, fast-growing, resource-consuming business; but is it wise? Union-Carbide's decision to not compensate the victims of the 1986 Bhopal disaster may have been smart for the business and stockholders; but was it wise? It takes a lot of smarts to win in the stock market or to close on a lucrative deal. Yet, as I write, the

Dow Jones keeps surpassing its own record highs and we are experiencing a partial government shut-down; Wall Street loves the massive layoffs, but average people are suffering. All smart, perhaps; but what of wisdom?

Wisdom considers past, present, and future.

Wisdom considers past, present, and future and results from reverence and appreciation. When you revere something you honor and respect it. When you appreciate something you grasp its inherent nature, its worth and significance. You experience reverence and appreciation through grace and humility; one way you can express it is through service.

Elders often would be among the last people to call themselves elders. "Elder" is a term of reverence and appreciation for the wisdom of one who has lived life and brings its resulting wisdom to the rest of us. In Native American tradition, the role of elder is a mantle bestowed by others upon those deemed worthy of carrying the responsibility. One cannot bestow it upon oneself. Yet, elders willingly receive the call to elderwork. Serving as an elder offers an opportunity to express in concrete terms the powers of reverence and appreciation.

Two questions I've pondered for years are "Where are all of *our* elders?" and "What *form* can and does 'elder' and 'elderwork' take in modern society and global business?" Some possibilities for leadership as elderwork are:

- Being present to what is needed in any given moment.
- Considering the past and the future, as well as the present.
- Modeling, though imperfectly like the rest of us, reverence, appreciation, humility and service within organizations and larger communities.
- Offering vision and spiritual wisdom without forcing it on others.
- Listening, arbitrating, and facilitating to gather wisdom.

- Continually questioning and challenging underlying myths and assumptions.
- Holding, maintaining, and reshaping business or society.
- Safeguarding essence and meaning with organizations and society.
- Helping to guide young people toward full, healthy, productive lives.
- Initiating and assisting others through life passages.
- Reminding the rest of us, in the midst of our hustle and bustle, of what is truly important and deserving of reverence and appreciation.

When the role of elder is insufficiently filled, all phases of our collective lives are, to some extent, neglected. Elders bring balance to the fast-paced, short-term orientation appropriate to our younger and middle years. Consider, for example, that the youth of any society are busy growing up, with all of the trials and tribulations finding their way in the world entails. Additionally, those of us in our middle years are busy moving through the time of building careers, developing deep and lasting relationships, raising families, and providing livelihood. We often have very little time or energy for thinking about the long term.

Elderwork is service beyond ego in support of the well-being and viability of the whole. It is a reciprocation for having had the fullness of youth and coming to the time beyond. Elderwork implies dropping the personal judgments about whether your experiences were "good" or "bad" and seeing that all that has happened in your life has contributed to the creation of your wisdom. Finally, in addition to being reciprocal, the elder time also offers you more than full "payment" through the satisfaction of service. As one elder, Albert Schweitzer, said, "You will never be happy until you have found a way to serve."

Elders are not to be confused with charismatic leaders or heroes; they can be highly visible or go completely unnoticed. With his involvement in Habitat for Humanity and international diplomacy in the years since the end of his term as president of the United States, Jimmy Carter has emulated the role of elder and the value of elderwork.

An elder may or may not be old chronologically. Wendy Luhabe of South Africa is a young elder. She established her business, Bridging the Gap, on the Zulu word *ubuntu*, which conveys the idea of honoring a person's humanity. Bridging the Gap helps prepare young black South Africans to enter the world of work. At 38, Luhabe sits on the boards of seven major corporations; last year she founded the country's first women's investment portfolio, to help alleviate the limited economic opportunities for black South African women.

No one is too young or too busy to serve. Through service we model and prepare for elderwork. It matters little what form it takes or what amount you give. What matters is *how* you give. What matters is your appreciative and reverent reciprocity for the gift of your life. As another of our great elders, Mother Theresa, expresses it, "Small things with great love. It is not how much we do, but how much love we put into the doing. It is not how much we give, but how much love we put in the giving."

Honoring Mystery

Think back to my experience of seeing my live blood on video—or perhaps your baby's ultrasound. How does a cell divide? How does it happen that a child resembles her parents? We know so much yet we know so little; we have barely touched the veneer of the mystery of life. As Einstein said, "The most beautiful thing we can experience is the mysterious. It is the source of all true art and science. He to whom this emotion is a stranger, who no longer pauses to wonder and stand rapt in awe, is as good as dead."

The mystery of life is ours both to behold and to hold. Sometimes the mystery is concrete and unique; sometimes humans can take some credit for it. In July 1989, on the twentieth anniversary of the first human walking on the moon, archive footage of the event was rebroadcast on television. I remember looking up at the moon outside my screen porch, asking myself, "Did it really happen? How was it possible?" It is amazing to imagine human beings in a small metal compartment flying as though from a slingshot through all of that black space and getting to exactly where they wanted to go. It's more amazing to imagine them coming back like a boomerang. Even more amazing is having them come back when something goes terribly wrong, as happened with *Apollo 13*. It was the mystery of conscious human creativity that got the crew home safely.

Sometimes the mystery is so subtle and common as to be taken for granted. Humans—and all life—are a result of that subtlety. A geography professor from graduate school once said, "Reality on earth is a condition of the temperature of the planet." Air, water, plants, animals, earth: all working and living together, all because the temperature of the planet is in a range that supports our forms of life, all because these particular forms of life have evolved to support each other. The whole living earth, the *Gaia* system, is taking form, living in symbiosis and homeostasis in the way it does, all because of the temperature of the planet.

There is inexpressible power in noticing the pervasiveness of the mystery, its exquisite nature, and of living in awe and honor as a result. Reverence is a gentle, quiet force of unfathomable magnitude.

Part III

The Well-Walked Path

PRELUDE

An Abode of Eternal Truth

For the human spirit caught within a spinning universe in an ever-confusing flow of events, circumstance and inner turmoil, to seek truth has always been to seek the invariable... To enter a temple constructed wholly of invariable geometric proportions is to enter an abode of eternal truth.

—Robert Lawlor

175

Geometric Perfection
Eight Powers and Seven Chakras
The Relationships of the Powers

Geometric Perfection

The temperature of our planet determines the milieu in which we live. It creates conditions that form our reality, in the same way water forms ocean reality for fish. Since we live within it, we tend not to notice it. We don't *need* to notice it—unless it is threatened. It is a natural gift that gives birth to, affects, and evolves conditions supporting life.

Our world abounds with fundamental and awesome conditions of perfection. The sun rises every morning; the seasons change regularly; the tides come in and go out, connected to the phases of the moon. From these kinds of natural phenomena humans have developed a language of order to describe and predict cyclical patterns of changing. That language is called "geometry," which means "measure of the earth." Geometry studies and describes spatial order by measuring and showing the relationships within and between forms.

In ancient Egypt the Nile flooded every year, washing away everything from the boundaries of farmland to the floor plans of temples and the paths between places. But the waters always receded, forming a basic cyclical pattern of flood and no flood. Each year, when the waters withdrew into the confines of the river's banks, the re-establishment of human-made boundaries, floor plans, and paths began again. As Lawlor says in *Sacred Geometry*, "This work was called geometry and was seen as a re-establishment of the principle of order and law on earth... This activity of 'measuring the earth' became the basis for a science of natural law..." (p. 6).

We don't have to go to the magnitude of the earth, seasons, and floods, however, to see the magnificence of geometric relationships. An everyday example we all embody—yet which is so often taken for granted as to be easily missed, except perhaps by artists—is the geometric relationships within our bodies.

Leonardo da Vinci's well-known drawing *Proportions of the Human Body* spatially shows the relationships of the human body to both the square and the circle. A square or cube is formed when we stand with our feet together and extend our arms straight out. By extending our arms up at an angle and separating our feet, we create a circle or sphere. All aspects of our bodies

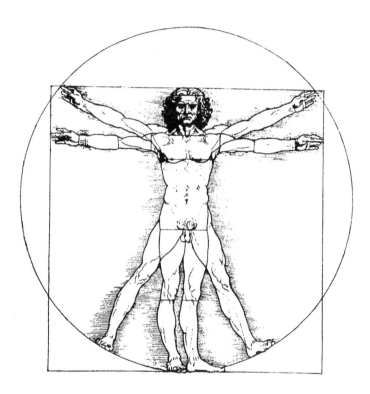

da Vinci's
Proportions of the Human Body

are mathematically related—even the smallest of bones in a finger—one to another. These relationships *within* our bodies also are proportional to patterns that characterize everything *outside* us, much the way the shape of a nautilus shell and a spiral galaxy are mathematically of similar proportions to each other. Thus, even mathematically we walk *within* and we walk *with*.

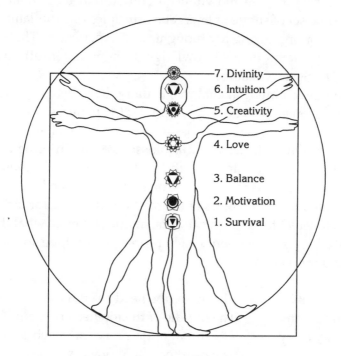

7. Divinity
6. Intuition
5. Creativity
4. Love
3. Balance
2. Motivation
1. Survival

The Seven Chakras

Eight Powers and Seven Chakras

You and I have each entered "a temple constructed wholly of invariable geometric proportions" by being born into physical bodies. At the same time that these abodes we live in may be physically temporary, they are also examples of immaculate, replicating geometric perfection. In addition to the geometric perfection we can see, much that is subtle, deep, and often unrecognized resides within and around each and every one of these bodies of ours.

There are any number of organizing principles from various traditions that can describe the eight personal powers of leadership since they collectively are the natural result and fulfillment of universal life force and vitality. In order to focus, I wanted to choose one set of subtle or energetic principles as a fundamental bedrock for organizing my thoughts and experiences. Though I have only a layperson's knowledge of them, my intuition led me to The Seven Chakras.

These seven internal chakras, usually described as rotating vortices of energy—one way we mirror the patterns of nautilus shells and galaxies—receive, assimilate, and transmit life energy or vitality. Often drawn as lotus blossoms with differing numbers of petals—from four for the first chakra to one thousand for the seventh chakra—they are often also described as having colors that match the colors of the rainbow, from red for the first chakra to violet for the seventh. One interpretation of what these geometric spirals of energy each represent and their locations within our bodies are:

7.	Divinity	The top of the head or crown
6.	Intuition	The middle of the forehead or medulla
5.	Creativity	The throat or first cervical vertebra
4.	Love	The heart or fifth thoracic vertebra
3.	Balance	The solar plexus or third lumbar vertebra
2.	Motivation	The last bone of spine or sacral vertebra
1.	Survival	The base of the spine or coccyx

The eight powers described throughout Part II of the book are built on the ancient wisdom of the seven chakras. Though the chakras are numerically labeled here, they are not separate, linear, or hierarchically arranged. Instead, all of the energies are essential, and of equal value; together they create a whole.

The seven chakras and the eight powers are related:

The path	The seven chakras	The eight powers
Within	1. Survival	1. Aliveness
Within	2. Motivation	2. Passion
Within	3. Balance	3. Integrity
Within	4. Love	4. Authenticity (love for self)
With	4. Love	4. Relatedness (love for others)
With	5. Creativity	5. Expression
With	6. Intuition	6. Perspective
With	7. Divinity	7. Reverence

The Relationships of the Powers

Using the seven chakras as a foundation, we can now look at the eight powers in relationship to each other. The first and most obvious relationship forms the organizational basis for Part II of this book. The first four chakras fundamentally underlie our walk within; and the second four chakras underlie our walk with each other. The fourth chakra, love, gets double duty, being in essence at the heart of interactions both within ourselves and with each other.

The relationships can be taken a step further and, with this deeper step, we return to numbers and perfection. By reversing the order of the second four powers and placing them parallel to the first powers, we see a new relationship between the powers of Walking Within and the powers of Walking With. Now each pair of powers, when matched with the traditional chakra numbers, adds to eight. In sacred geometry, the number eight represents perfect symmetry or balance, and, turned on its side, is the symbol for infinity.

Walking Within		Walking With		
1. Aliveness	+	7. Reverence	=	8
2. Passion	+	6. Perspective	=	8
3. Integrity	+	5. Expression	=	8
4. Authenticity	+	4. Relatedness	=	8

Thus, for example, the inner experience of aliveness can be broadcast through expressing reverence. The inner experience of passion can be informed by an expanded perspective. The inner experience of integrity can offer shape and contour to expression. And the inner experience of authenticity, of self-love, can make it possible for us to love each other and to know we are all related.

Connecting with the geometric and energetic perfection of the human design can give you concrete help in reaching deeply into your essence. It can also assist you in grounding or locating yourself in the universal order. It simultaneously helps you comprehend both your uniqueness and your commonality with all creation.

Chapter 15

Integrating the Eight Powers

Almost anything you do will seem insignificant but it is very important that you do it... You must be the change you wish to see in the world.

—Mahatma Gandhi

General Complementarity
Specific Balance
Forming a Whole

General Complementarity

A complementarity exists in the relationship between the two sets of four powers. To illustrate the distinctions between "With" and "Within," we can use the metaphor of different sources of light. Electricity is the generator, the "source"; it is the common, unifying factor behind many kinds of electrical light in the world. Yet, lights generated by electricity can look very different and serve different purposes.

We can use the halogen light as a metaphor for powers of Walking Within and the floodlight as a metaphor for Walking With. Halogen lights provide brilliant, intense light, highlighting a reading area or a piece of art. Floodlights, on the other hand, broadcast bright light over an expansive area allowing you to watch an evening high-school football game, or play broomball on an outdoor ice rink on a winter's night. The lights, though coming from the same original source, each give us something distinct. And, together, they complement each other. One offers intense focus on a localized area; the other offers light over an expanded area.

Two Sources of Light

So it is with the eight powers. The energy that rotates the chakras can be seen as the generator, the source; it is the unifying, common factor behind the light of vitality in life. Just as the light generated by electricity can serve very different purposes, the light-generating eight powers also serve different purposes.

While all eight powers come from the same original source, the first four are akin to the halogen lights. They are intensely focused on a localized area: Walking within is your individual inner life. The second four powers of Walking With are akin to the floodlight, demonstrating how your individual life and light is broadcast over an expansive range and is interwoven with all of life.

Specific Balance

Describing the eight powers of separate qualities, as stated earlier, is useful for purposes of articulation and description; but only together do they form a whole of balanced energy. As we look into a one-to-one relationship between arbitrarily divided powers within and powers with, every power actually balances and supports every other power. For example, aliveness supports and balances each of the other seven powers, and is supported and balanced by them. The same relationship exists for each of the other seven, supporting every other power and being supported by them.

To specifically illustrate how the chakras may serve as balance and support for each other, we will briefly explore the pairs that, together, add up to eight, the number of symmetry and balance.

Strength in excess can become a great weakness or liability.

In this context, balance is defined as bringing the scales of the two powers into equilibrium with each other. Part II describes the eight powers primarily in terms of the strengths of each; it is based on the assumption that growth in and development of each power is valuable, wise, and healing. Yet, strength in excess can become a great weakness and liability. It is possible to overextend each of the powers. It is also possible for the overextended "strengths" to be used in negative ways.

Hitler had enormous aliveness, passion, authenticity, and expression—but what of his reverence, perspective, relatedness, and integrity? He represents an archetype for four of the powers being overextended, with the other four being underdeveloped. And, in four pairs, the imbalances add up to eight:

Walking Within	Walking With
1. Aliveness	4. Relatedness
2. Passion	5. Expression
3. Integrity	6. Perspective
4. Authenticity	7. Reverence

Thus, one way of assessing for yourself where you need to develop your individual powers and where you need to establish balance is to pay attention to, and attend to, your imbalances. When one of a pair of powers becomes overextended, another can serve as its balance. Following, by way of example, is what an overextension of each power looks like and how the reciprocal power brings balance.

Walking Within	Walking With
1. **Aliveness**	4. Relatedness
2. Passion	5. Expression
3. Integrity	6. Perspective
4. Authenticity	7. **Reverence**

Reverence Balances Overextended Aliveness

Aliveness brings the strengths of full engagement, living in the present, and letting go. When aliveness is overextended, it results in self-centeredness and a "devil-may-care" attitude about the future. It does not prompt you to notice your connection to the cosmos and it does not take into account long-term needs, whether days or generations out. It means a giving in to fate because of feeling unable to shape or influence the present and future.

Balance is re-established by calling on the power of reverence. For example, place your attention on areas where you experience grace in your life. Ask yourself about your self-absorption and what it hides; you may be afraid to notice deep and true humility. Search out ways to serve. In whatever way nourishes you, immerse yourself in a blessed, mystical, ancient natural setting—whether physically or in your mind's eye.

Aliveness Balances Overextended Reverence

The strengths of reverence are honoring mystery, finding fulfilling service, and relishing experiences of grace and humility. These strengths become weaknesses when you submerge yourself so fully in awe that you feel personally diminished and inadequate in this grand universe. It is true that you are an infinitesimal grain of sand. But that does not mean that your individual life is in any way diminished or meaningless. Taken a step further, if you feel small and meaningless in relation to all, you may overcompensate by developing feelings of superiority and separateness from the rest of life. This same imbalance of self-importance has pervaded our culture for the last several hundred years; it has led us to think of ourselves as separate from, and superior to, the rest of the web of life.

Focusing on the miracle of your unique and perfect presence in the world at this time brings the overextended reverence into balance. Notice that, while life is often dangerous, you are currently safe. Notice the easy, average nature of this moment.

Decide to be fully here, now, reading these words. Deliberately seek ways to see and conquer your self-importance, exchanging it for coming to know more fully the nature of your unique aliveness—your talents and gifts.

Walking Within	**Walking With**
1. Aliveness	4. Relatedness
2. **Passion**	5. Expression
3. Integrity	6. **Perspective**
4. Authenticity	7. Reverence

Perspective Balances Overextended Passion

Becoming clear about your passion and purpose offers you the gifts of meaning, energy, and direction—all of which add up to momentum. Overextended passion takes the form of fanaticism, single-mindedness, and obsession; you become so purposeful that you no longer see other possibilities and become convinced there aren't any viable ones other than yours. Overextended passion leads to a "push" mentality of needing to convince everyone around you that you have the one right way. It causes you to be unable to hear the thoughts, passions, and needs of others, and makes it difficult for you to collaborate or find synergy.

Nothing you have, take meaning from, or find of value, lives in isolation.

At such times, call on the power of perspective. Perspective balances passion by recognizing that there is almost always more than one viable way to approach anything in life. When your passion is overextended, look for alternatives. Decide to build a bigger picture for yourself by enlarging your context. Develop a field of view by drawing in dissonant or foreign information and sifting through it for what is of value. Remember that nothing you have, take meaning from, or find of value, lives in isolation; that all you have, think, and are is connected to everything else.

Passion Balances Overextended Perspective

A primary strength of perspective is detachment. Detachment comes from thinking holistically, developing a field of view, and enlarging your context. Overextended perspective becomes a detachment from your feelings and from what "turns you on." Another strength of perspective is seeing alternatives which, when overextended, causes you to feel immobilized from having too many good choices. Together, the overextension of these strengths leads you to seeing broadly but without the ability to discern what matters to you or where you make a difference.

The power of passion re-establishes balance. Your passion assists you in choosing one direction among many—not just any one direction, but one that suits you and that you have motivation to follow. Passion balances perspective by bringing focus and appropriate scale for action to even the most global context. When seeking to balance perspective, ask yourself, "What am I really feeling, really wanting?" If nothing comes, notice how out of touch you are with your feelings, explore why that is, and determine how to regain contact with yourself. Assess your current relationship to your "life's work" and find ways to engage or re-engage in it more fully.

Walking Within	Walking With
1. Aliveness	4. Relatedness
2. Passion	5. **Expression**
3. **Integrity**	6. Perspective
4. Authenticity	7. Reverence

Expression Balances Overextended Integrity

The strengths of the power of integrity are certainty in your personal values, the courage to live them, and the congruence that comes as a result. Overextended integrity results from placing too much confidence in the rightness of your personal values. Integrity gone from strength to weakness shows itself as righteousness, rigidity, and moral superiority. It leads you to self-deception and an inability to examine your beliefs and assumptions.

Balance comes through the power of expression. Expression is based on speaking truth and learning. It is evidence of creation. Remember that you are designed to learn and create; that everyday is a new day in which to begin again. Everyday you receive new information and affirm your life and values all over again. Thus, everyday you have the opportunity to change them as well. Consider the life of a snake. The snake's skin defines its boundaries and holds it together, gives it integrity. But with some regularity, the snake sheds its skin. That former identity is too small to handle the snake's expansion.

Integrity Balances Overextended Expression

Strengths of the power of expression are knowing and speaking your personal truth and bringing your creative ideas into form. The power of expression becomes overextended through the gathering of power over others or at the expense of others. Expression of personal truth, when out of balance, becomes undue influence and control. Expression is also overextended when "doing" becomes an attempt to satisfy or legitimate "being."

When you introduce the power of integrity as a means of balancing expression, you may find yourself looking starkly into how your personal presence and truth may be "doing unto others what you would *never* want done unto you." Explore the "why" behind your doing and test it against what you *say* are your personal values. Ask yourself whether your essence or being supports your doing or whether you might be doing as a way to legitimate—both to yourself and others—your being in the world. Remind yourself that your being in the world is a "done deal"; no specific doing or amount of achievement is required.

Walking Within	Walking With
1. Aliveness	4. **Relatedness**
2. Passion	5. Expression
3. Integrity	6. Perspective
4. **Authenticity**	7. Reverence

Relatedness Balances Overextended Authenticity

Authenticity brings you the strengths of inner wisdom, internally centered guidance, and a quality of peace with yourself. Yet, when overextended, individual authenticity or autonomy becomes an illusion of independence and a need for control. Being independent and having a sense of some control in your life are valuable assets. At times, they keep you alive. In excess, however, they lead you into isolation.

The power of relatedness brings balance through reintroducing you to your connectedness. It rejoins you to the university of the human condition. Draw on the power of relatedness to help you remember the gifts of vulnerability and compassion. Risk re-experiencing the peace and joy that comes from being seen and "held" by another, from taking the earth off of your shoulders and allowing yourself to receive support.

Authenticity Balances Overextended Relatedness

Strengths of the power of relatedness include your abilities to work well with others, to experience empathy and compassion for others' needs, and to engage deeply with them. When overextended, the power of relatedness exhibits the weaknesses of co-dependence and excessive dependence. Co-dependence, simply put, means, "You matter more than I do." While we *are* dependent upon each other, dependence to excess means, "I need you in order to survive."

The power of authenticity allows you to "return home" to yourself, your inner life and inner knowing. With authenticity you introduce balance by remembering to be loyal to your own needs along with those of others. Remember that true giving comes from a place of peace and wisdom and from first giving to yourself. Remember that all relationships are temporary; deep within the well of yourself you are alone and have your own ability to survive.

Forming a Whole

Once again, we return to the *Tai Ji* symbol of yin and yang. Developing your powers has no beginning and no end; these powers are eternally dynamic. Each flows into all the others. Together in their relationships with each other, they express your core, your essence. You have access to all of them, no matter how fully they currently may be developed or known to you.

The choices and decisions you make daily as you lead in this challenging world of ours demonstrate both your level of development and level of balance and integration of eight powers within you. Those moments when you notice that all eight come into balance and seem to interact seamlessly with and in support of each other are moments when you come to know your deep capacity for leading in a sacred manner. The more those moments happen, the more they are likely to happen again.

Chapter 16

Walk Well

It comes back to each one of you...to really commit yourselves to making all humanity a success...

—BUCKMINSTER FULLER

Accepting Responsibility
Life as Paradox
Our Evolutionary Process
Facing Unanswerable Questions

Accepting Responsibility

Given the complex dilemmas, the pace of life, and the magnitude
of change you face as a business leader on the threshold of the
twenty-first century, you must be open to changing beliefs and
assumptions. You must be open to taking unprecedented risks by
making decisions that serve not only your own business but also
serve life—if we are to have a world in which to do business in
the future.

If you do not acknowledge your power for shaping the future,
who else is there? Only a small portion of the world's population
has the luxury you and I have. I, for example, have enough extra
energy to write a book; you have money to buy it and time to read
it. Our daily needs are being met.

Once you become aware of the times in which we live and the
challenges facing us, it is difficult, if not impossible, to ignore
your sacred responsibility. Yet you pay a bittersweet price for
being among the wealthiest of human beings on earth and for
participating in the powerful arena of business. It is the price of
awareness.

While traveling in Kenya, some Australian friends and I
stopped our Land Rover by the side of the road so the children
could have a stretch break. The sun shone hot. The silence on the
savanna was complete except for a whistling wind that made
waves of the tall, brown grasses.

In the distance a shepherd tended his sheep. Knowing nothing
about him, I nonetheless felt romance about his life because it
appeared so idyllic, peaceful, and free from global cares. Then I
felt a sense of loss; because of my own global frame of reference,

I realized that I could never get to where he is because of what I know and have experienced. In contrast, while working in The Sudan, I watched Ethiopian women leave the refugee camp early in the morning to spend their entire day walking miles, scrounging enough wood to cook the evening meal. Their lives appeared to be such a struggle, so resigned, so full of burdens. Realizing I didn't want to ever get to where they were, I felt gratitude for all I know and have experienced; for my global frame of reference.

The price of awareness is enormous but it is not necessarily a sacrifice.

The price of awareness is enormous but it is not necessarily a sacrifice. Much is demanded of you, because you have the capacity to contribute and because you are a leader in business. This will be especially true in the next ten to twenty years. For paying the price, you will receive in return the priceless gift of your own growth and evolution, your own greater consciousness and connectedness.

As a leader in the powerful arena of business, you are responsible for our larger community—beyond Wall Street and stockholders. As Leon Shenandoah of the Six Nations Iroquois Confederacy said, "These are our times and our responsibilities. Every human being has a sacred duty to protect the welfare of our Mother Earth, from whom all life comes. In order to do this we must recognize the enemy—the one within us. We must begin with ourselves...." In his book *In the Absence of the Sacred*, Jerry Mander recounts the disaster at the Union Carbide plant in Bhopal, India. About 200,000 people were injured; 2,000 died. Immediately following the accident the chairman of Union Carbide, deeply upset by what had happened, told the media that he would do whatever was necessary to make up for the losses people had experienced. Yet a year later, the same person said he had overreacted—and was going to lead the legal fight *not* to pay damages.

How had this executive come to terms with what appears to be a shift from being an authentically grief-stricken and compassionate human being to assuming the role of a "hard-nosed" business person? It appears he merely allowed himself to be victim to our collectively held beliefs about what it takes to be a good business leader, about what is required to make a business successful. Collectively shared yet unexplored, unchallenged assumptions of "business" determined the outcome of this incident.

While the magnitude or gravity of the decisions we face may seem less for you and me, we each must make decisions that impact the lives of others every day. No matter what situation you find yourself in, there are only three choices; you can adapt, you can influence others, or you can leave. Thus, you need to be well prepared to respond in ways that *serve* when you are cast into despairing and apparently no-win situations. You need a deep personal foundation that is highly integrated with whatever form is taken by your own spirituality, your connection to a higher power.

Your personal, sacred work as a leader is to come into greater harmony with the natural flow of life; to join the river and enjoy the ride, only damming or dredging when it is absolutely essential. But how to determine when to let go, and when to take action? You must hold the tensions of paradox that are within all of life. The tensions, for example, of what is going-to-happen-in-any-case and what is choice, of what you *perceive* to be real and what is true. You must think anew, feel anew. You can only accomplish this by challenging and growing what is within you.

Life as Paradox

In reading my seventh-story dream in the Prelude to Part I, your first reaction might have been to judge those on the seventh story for not doing something to care for the masses outside the gate. It most certainly was mine. Yet, there is a paradox here. As a fire may be both destructive and creative, the paradox in the dream relates to letting go. It is difficult to allow ourselves to *be* in the natural order of life. Many of us on the seventh story want to control. We know how to control. We feel safer and more successful when we are in control.

Even the concept of "global sustainability" presumes that if we can get control of ourselves, our inventions, and our technology, we can create a better world. Yet attempting to prevent or control natural processes is out of harmony. It breaks the whole of life apart. It may work temporarily, even for decades or centuries; but ultimately, it is not life supporting. It eventually results in suffering and struggle.

In the realm of creativity, as human beings we often are forced to notice our illusions of control. Every astronaut, especially in the early days of space flight, had to let go. Nothing was assured. He had to prepare for his death in order to be "reborn" in weightlessness, and then had to let go again in order to be "reborn" on the return to earth's gravity.

In July of 1995 the crews of *Mir* and *Atlantis*, so recently enemies and competitors, were having their first party together in space. Their accomplishment illustrates how quickly whole systems can change, how beautifully we can create, how far we can reach when our attention is deliberate and conscious. The docking of those two space vehicles demonstrates both profound human ingenuity and talent along with forgiveness and collaboration.

Yet, the dark dot on the light side of the *Tai Ji* symbol signifies, for example, how the shuttle missions study the fragile state of life support systems on earth. They measure the ozone hole as it grows. They watch for fires and other signs of deforestation. They track changing weather patterns. The products of that awesome creativity are recording the dying process of life forms on our planet, while avoiding a junkyard of orbiting space-program debris. They are witnessing where our attention is accidental and unconscious.

Our Evolutionary Process

As with the dots in the *Tai Ji* symbol, if you cling too tightly to what is dying, if you miss opportunities to explore the emerging creative, you may hinder your own evolution. It is the very nature of the universe in general, and the human design in particular, to create and evolve.

Seeing the wholeness of earth without political boundaries, set alone in the blackness of space, is changing what it means to be a human being.

When creativity is out of balance with natural law, the results can be disastrous. Nuclear waste is the result of creativity, yes, but without accordance for harmony with all of life. When creativity is in balance with natural law, the results can be evolutionary. Seeing the wholeness of earth without political boundaries, set alone in the blackness of space, is quite literally changing what it means to be a human being.

My hope is kindled daily as I notice more and more people in business acknowledging the dilemmas we face. My hope also is kindled as more and more people bring soul and spirit, personal wholeness and deep purpose, to work with them. We can support each other in grasping our sacred work as leaders, no matter what is going on outside of us. Adding to that, we can support each other in seizing our opportunity to lead well at this critical juncture in evolution on earth.

Our collective hope lies in our ongoing evolution. At times of greatest transformation, conditions often seem to get worse before they get better. The more we explicitly address our beliefs, the greater our likelihood of evolving our metaphoric gills into lungs.

Facing Unanswerable Questions

This book is not about saving the earth. The earth can take care of itself. This book is about saving ourselves. It is about coming more fully into harmony with all of life—our own, each other's, the animals, the plants.

As you journey on your path of providing leadership in the world today, you must face into the polarities and live with the open question about what of the forest is dying and what is being born. You must be willing to hold the tension of exploring how these apparent opposites together make a whole, how they are parts of the same life cycle.

As you develop more of the capacity for which you are designed, you will access more of the potential available to you. If you focus on how you can see the garden in a whole new way, you will creatively and collaboratively find yourself doing things you previously thought could not be done in places you never thought you could do them, with effects you never thought you could achieve.

At the same time, a real and daunting possibility we face is that the momentum of global forces is beyond positive human impact, beyond repair; that even supporting the natural flow of evolution within your life, doing your best to lead consciously and conscientiously, bringing soul and spirit to work, is not enough; that changing systems is not enough; that the fire of the dream is destruction and it is headed our way; that whether or not we close the curtains, it will consume us right along with everything and everybody else.

All life in the forest has its cycles of birth, growth, death. So it is with the forest itself. Perhaps we have the unusual opportunity of witnessing the dying forest, the death of biological life on earth. A powerful resource for contemplating this possibility is a work of art called *The Box: Remembering the Gift*. It is in fact a beautiful wooden box, containing portfolios developed over several years by five artists and authors. The first portfolio is the "Book of Sorrow"; within it is the folio "Ecocide." The authors invite us to notice that the death of life on earth is not unique. It has happened before. It is natural. Then, if we perhaps live in such a time, the question arises: "How do I want to live in a dying time?"

One Friday a group of dear friends spent the evening together. We go deep whenever we are together. One woman said, "I just came from the doctor because this morning I found a lump in my breast. The doctor thinks it's benign, but I won't know the results until next week." We talked of times when we each thought we might be facing death. What we shared were experiences of exquisite aliveness and presence, gratitude, deep grief, review and reflection, connection, desire to do what is as yet undone; most of all we shared the growth and healing that occurs during those times. Perhaps facing directly into the possibility that *Gaia*, the whole system of life on earth, is dying, offers us a collective time of exquisite aliveness and presence, gratitude, deep grief, review and reflection, connection, doing what is as yet undone, and growth and healing.

Changing systems to create a viable future on one hand, and witnessing the death of life on the other, are apparently opposite. Yet, while accepting both as fully possible, I have discovered that whichever shows itself to be most likely in the next few years, my relationship to my work and purpose remains consistent. It is unaltered. Like beadwork, the sizes, shapes, and colors of the beads may differ and be used to form very different designs from one garment to another. But the thread that connects them remains constant.

Believing one way or the other about whether the forest will continue as it is—whether it is dying wholesale, or whether instead we are passing through the birth canal to a whole new reality—does not ultimately matter. In each scenario, what is at stake is the quality of *your* life, of *my* life; the experience of the present and being fully present in our lives as they unfold; the fullness of our growth, creativity, and healing; and our relatedness to all life.

To lead originally meant to set out on a quest, to navigate into the distant horizon. I seek to lead by walking well on the path as it presents itself and wish the same for you.

Bibliography

The following is an eclectic list of readings, mostly books, that have supported my journey and affected my thinking. All are woven into the fabric of this book. The ones marked with * are directly referred to in the text.

Adams, Scott. *The Dilbert Principle: A Cubicle's-Eye View of Bosses, Meetings, Management Fads & Other Workplace Afflictions.* New York, NY: HarperBusiness, 1996.

Anthony, Dick, Bruce Ecker, and Ken Wilber, eds. *Spiritual Choices: The Problem of Recognizing Authentic Paths to Inner Transformation.* New York: Paragon House Publishers, 1987.

*Arrien, Angeles. *The Four-Fold Way: Walking the Paths of the Warrior, Teacher, Healer and Visionary.* San Francisco, CA: HarperSanFrancisco, 1993.

Autry, James A. *Love and Profit: The Art of Caring Leadership.* New York: William Morrow and Company, Inc., 1991.

Baldwin, Christina. *Calling the Circle: The First and Future Culture.* Newberg, OR: Swan/Raven & Co., 1994.

Barks, Coleman, trans. *The Essential Rumi.* San Francisco, CA: HarperSanFrancisco, 1995.

Bateson, Mary Catherine. *Composing a Life.* New York: Penguin Plume, 1989.

Bennis, Warren, and Burt Nanus. *Leaders: The Strategies for Taking Charge.* New York: Harper & Row, 1985.

*Bernbaum, Edwin. *The Way to Shambhala.* New York, NY: Anchor Press/Doubleday, 1980.

Bernstein, Albert J., and Sydney Craft Rozen. *Sacred Bull: The Inner Obstacles That Hold You Back at Work and How to Overcome Them.* New York: John Wiley & Sons, Inc., 1994.

*Berry, Thomas. *The Dream of the Earth.* San Francisco, CA: Sierra Club Books, 1988.

Block, Peter. *Stewardship: Choosing Service Over Self-Interest.* San Francisco, CA: Berrett-Koehler, 1993.

*Blum, Ralph. *The Book of Runes.* New York: St. Martin's Press, 1982.

Bohm, David and Mark Edwards. *Changing Consciousness: Exploring the Hidden Source of the Social, Political and Environmental Crises Facing our World.* San Francisco, CA: HarperSanFrancisco, 1991.

Bohm, David. *On Dialogue.* Ojai, CA: David Bohm Seminars, 1990.

_____. *Wholeness and the Implicate Order.* London: Ark Paperbacks, 1992.

Bolman, Lee G. and Terrence E. Deal. *Leading with Soul: An Uncommon Journey of Spirit.* San Francisco, CA: Jossey-Bass, 1995.

*Breton, Denise, and Christopher Largent. *The Soul of Economies: Spiritual Evolution Goes to the Marketplace.* Wilmington, DE: Idea House Publishing Company, 1991.

Bridges, William. *JobShift: How to Prosper in a Workplace Without Jobs.* Reading, MA: Addison-Wesley Publishing, 1994.

*Bridges, William. *Surviving Corporate Transition: Rational Management in a World of Mergers, Layoffs, Start-ups, Divestitures, Deregulation, and New Technologies.* New York: Doubleday, 1988.

Bruyere, Rosalyn L. *Wheels of Light: Chakras, Auras, and the Healing Energy of the Body.* New York: Simon and Schuster, 1994.

*Burnett, Frances Hodgson. *The Secret Garden.* New York: Lippincott, 1985.

Caldicott, Helen. *If You Love This Planet: A Plan to Heal the Earth.* New York: W. W. Norton & Company, 1992.

Cameron, Julia. *The Artist's Way: A Spiritual Path to Higher Creativity.* New York: Jeremy P. Tarcher/Perigee, 1992.

*Campbell, Joseph. *Hero With a Thousand Faces.* Second ed. Princeton, NJ: Princeton University Press, 1971.

Carey, Ken. *Return of the Bird Tribes.* San Francisco, CA: Harper SanFrancisco, 1988.

Carey, Ken. *Starseed, The Third Millenium: Living a the Posthistoric World.* San Francisco, CA: HarperSanFrancisco, 1991.

*Carlin, Peter. "How to Make a Decision Like a Tribe." *Fast Company*, Premier Issue, 1996.

Carlson, Don and Craig Comstock, eds. *Securing Our Planet: How to Succeed When Threats Are Too Risky and There's Really No Defense.* Los Angeles, CA: Jeremy P. Tarcher, Inc., 1986.

Chappell, Tom. *The Soul of a Business: Managing for Profit and the Common Good.* New York: Bantam Books, 1993.

Chopra, Deepak. *Ageless Body, Timeless Mind: The Quantum Alternative to Growing Old,* New York: Harmony Books, 1993.

*_____. *The Seven Spiritual Laws of Success: A Practical Guide to the Fulfillment of Your Dreams.* San Raphael, CA: New World Library, 1994.

Collins, James C., and Jerry I. Porras. *Built to Last: Successful Habits of Visionary Companies.* New York: HarperBusiness, 1994.

Covey, Stephen R. *The Seven Habits of Highly Effective People.* New York: Simon and Schuster, 1989.

Daly, Herman E., and John B. Cobb, Jr. *For the Common Good: Redirecting the Economy Toward Community, the Environment, and a Sustainable Future.* Boston, MA: Beacon Press, 1989.

Das, Ram and Paul Gorman. *How Can I Help? Stories and Reflections on Service.* New York: Alfred A. Knopf, 1988.

DePree, Max. *Leadership Is an Art.* New York: Dell Publishing, 1989.

Devall, Bill. *Simple in Means, Rich in Ends: Practicing Deep Ecology.* Salt Lake City, UT: Gibbs Smith, 1988.

_____, and George Sessions. *Deep Ecology: Living as if Nature Mattered.* Salt Lake City, UT: Gibbs Smith, 1985.

DiCarlo, Russell E. *Towards a New World View: Conversations at the Leading Edge.* Erie, PA: Epic Publishing, 1996.

Dossey, Larry. *Healing Words: The Power of Prayer and the Practice of Medicine.* San Francisco, CA: HarperSanFrancisco, 1993.

Easwaran, Eknath. *Take Your Time: Finding Balance in a Hurried World.* Berkeley, CA: Nilgiri Press, 1994.

Elliott, William. *Tying Rocks to Clouds: Meetings and Conversations with Wise and Spiritual People.* New York: Doubleday, 1996.

Feinstein, David, and Stanley Krippner. *Personal Mythology: The Psychology of Your Evolving Self.* Los Angeles, CA: Jeremy P. Tarcher, Inc., 1988.

Feng, Gia-fu, and Jerome Kirk. *Tai Chi—A Way of Centering & I Ching.* New York: Collier Books, 1970.

Fideler, David. *Jesus Christ Sun of God: Ancient Cosmology and Early Christian Symbolism.* Wheaton, IL: Quest Books, 1993.

Fields, Rick, Peggy Taylor, Rex Weyler, and Rick Ingrasci. *Chop Wood Carry Water: A Guide to Finding Spiritual Fulfillment in Everyday Life.* Los Angeles, CA: Jeremy P. Tarcher, Inc., 1984.

Fox, Matthews. *The Reinvention of Work: A New Vision for Livelihood for Our Time.* San Francisco, CA: HarperSanFrancisco, 1994.

*Fox, Robert W. "The World's Urban Explosion." *National Geographic,* August 1984.

*Frissell, Bob. *Nothing in this Book Is True, But It's Exactly How Things Are.* Berkeley, CA: Frog, Ltd., 1994.

Fritz, Robert. *Creating.* New York: Fawcett Columbine, 1991.

Garfield, Charles. *Second to None: How Our Smartest Companies Put People First.* Homewood, IL: Business One Irwin, 1992.

Goleman, Daniel. *Emotional Intelligence: Why It Can Matter More Than IQ.* New York: Bantam Books, 1995.

Gore, Albert R., Jr. *Earth in the Balance: Ecology and the Human Spirit.* Boston, MA: Houghton Mifflin Company, 1992.

Hancock, Graham. *Lords of Poverty: The Power, Prestige, and Corruption of the International Aid Business.* New York: Atlantic Monthly Press, 1989.

Handy, Charles. *The Age of Unreason.* Boston, MA: Harvard Business School Press, 1989.

Hanh, Thich Nhat. *The Blooming of a Lotus: Guided Meditation Exercises for Healing and Transformation.* Boston, MA: Beacon Press, 1993.

*Harman, Willis. *Global Mind Change: The Promise of the Last Years of the Twentieth Century.* Indianapolis, IN: Knowledge Systems, Inc., 1988.

_____, and John Hormann. *Creative Work: The Constructive Role of Business in a Transforming Society.* Indianapolis, IN: Knowledge Systems, Inc., 1990.

_____, and Howard Rheingold. *Higher Creativity: Liberating the Unconscious for Breakthrough Insights.* Los Angeles, CA: Jeremy P. Tarcher, Inc., 1984.

Hawken, Paul. *The Ecology of Commerce: A Declaration of Sustainability.* New York: HarperBusiness, 1993.

Hawley, Jack. *Reawakening the Spirit in Work: The Power of Dharmic Management.* San Francisco, CA: Berrett-Koehler, 1993.

Heider, John. *The Tao of Leadership: Leadership Strategies for a New Age.* New York: Bantam Books, 1985.

Henderson, Hazel. *Paradigms in Progress: Life Beyond Economics.* Indianapolis, IN: Knowledge Systems, Inc., 1991.

*Hock, Dee W. *The Chaordic Organization: Out of Control and Into Order.* World Business Academy Perspectives, Volume 9, Number 1; Berrett-Koehler, San Francisco, CA, 1995.

Huang, Chungliang Al, and Jerry Lynch. *Mentoring: The TAO of Giving and Receiving Wisdom.* San Francisco, CA: HarperSanFrancisco, 1995.

Hubbard, Barbara Marx. *The Revelation: A Message of Hope for the New Millennium.* Novato, CA: Nataraj Publishing, 1995.

*_____. *The Revelation: Our Crisis Is a Birth.* Greenbrae, CA: Foundation for Conscious Evolution, 1993.

Inamori, Kazuo. *A Passion for Success: Practical, Inspirational, and Spiritual Insight from Japan's Leading Entrepreneur.* New York: McGraw-Hill, Inc., 1995.

Ingerman, Sandra. *Welcome Home: Following Your Soul's Journey Home.* San Francisco, CA: HarperSanFrancisco, 1993.

Ingram, Catherine. *In the Footsteps of Gandhi: Conversations with Spiritual Social Activists.* Berkeley, CA: Parallax Press, Berkeley, 1990.

Jacobs, Robert W. *Real Time Strategic Change: How to Involve an Entire Organization in Fast and Far-Reaching Change.* San Francisco, CA: Berrett-Koehler, 1994.

Johnston, Charles M. *The Creative Imperative: A Four-Dimensional Theory of Human Growth & Planetary Evolution.* Berkeley, CA: Celestial Arts, 1986.

Kabat-Zinn, Jon. *Wherever You Go There You Are: Mindfulness Meditation in Everyday Life.* New York: Hyperion, 1994.

*Kaplan, Robert D. "The Coming Anarchy." *Atlantic Monthly*, February 1994.

Kay, James J. and Eric Schneider. "Embracing Complexity: The Challenge of the Ecosystem Approach." *Alternatives*, Volume 20, Number 3. 1994.

*Kelley, Colleen, Robert Ott, Marlow Hodgekiss, Gigi Coyle, and Parvati Narcus. *The Box: Remembering the Gift.* Santa Fe, NM: The Terma Company, 1992.

Kelley, Kevin W. (for the Association of Space Explorers). *The Home Planet*. Reading, MA: Addison-Wesley, 1988.

*Kelly, Marjorie. "The Rising Storm: To Transform Our Economic System, Crisis May Be Necessary." *Business Ethics*, November /December 1995.

*Korten, David C.. *Getting to the 21st Century: Voluntary Action and the Global Agenda*. West Hartford, CT: Kumarian Press, 1990.

_____. *When Corporations Rule the World*. San Francisco, CA, and West Hartford, CT: Berrett-Koehler/Kumerian Press, 1995.

Kyle, David T. *Human Robots & Holy Mechanics: Reclaiming Our Souls in a Machine World*. Portland, OR: Swan/Raven & Company, 1993.

Kubler-Ross, Elisabeth. *Death: The Final Stage of Growth*. Englewood Cliffs, NJ: Prentice-Hall, Inc., 1975.

Land, George and Beth Jarman. *Breakpoint and Beyond: Mastering the Future—Today*. New York: HarperBusiness, 1992.

*Lawlor, Robert. *Sacred Geometry: Philosophy and Practice*. London: Thames and Hudson, Ltd., 1982.

Leakey, Richard and Roger Lewin. *Patterns of Life and the Future of Humankind*. New York: Doubleday, 1996.

*LeGuin, Ursula K. *A Wizard of Earthsea*. New York: Bantam Books, 1980.

LeShan, Lawrence. *How to Meditate: A Guide to Self-Discovery*. New York: Bantam Books, 1975.

Liebig, James E. *Merchants of Vision: People Bringing New Purpose and Values to Business*. San Francisco, CA: Berrett-Koehler, 1994.

*Llosa, Mario Vargas. *The Storyteller*. New York: Penguin Books, 1989.

Lodge, George C. *Managing Globalization in the Age of Interdependence*. San Diego, CA: Pfeiffer & Company, 1995.

*Loeb, Marshall. "Editor's Desk: Listen to Business Leaders Talk About Leadership." *Fortune*, 14 December 1992.

Lovelock, James. *The Ages of Gaia: A Biography of Our Living Earth*. New York: W.W. Norton and Company, 1988.

Lulic, Margaret A. *Who We Could Be at Work*. Newton, MA: Butterworth–Heinemann, 1996.

MacNeill, Jim, Pieter Winsemius, and Taizo Yakushiji. *Beyond Interdependence: The Meshing of the World's Economy and the Earth's Ecology*. New York: Oxford University Press, 1991.

Macy, Joanna. *Despair and Personal Power in the Nuclear Age.* Philadelphia, PA: New Society Publishers, 1983.

*Mander, Jerry. *In the Absence of the Sacred: The Failure of Technology & the Survival of the Indian Nations.* San Francisco, CA: Sierra Club Books, 1991.

McKibben, Bill. *Hope, Human and Wild: True Stories of Living Lightly on the Earth.* Boston, MA: Little Brown and Company, 1995.

Menzel, Peter. *Material World: A Global Family Portrait.* San Francisco, CA: Sierra Club Books, 1994.

Mindell, Arnold. *The Leader as Martial Artist: An Introduction to Deep Democracy.* San Francisco, CA: HarperSanFrancisco, 1992.

_____. *The Year I, Global Process Work: Community Creation from Global Problems, Tensions and Myths.* London: Arkana, 1989.

Mitchell, Stephen. *Tao Te Ching.* New York: Harper & Row, 1988.

Moran, Robert T., Philip R. Harris, and William G. Stripp. *Developing the Global Organization: Strategies for Human Resource Professionals.* Houston, TX: Gulf Publishing, 1993.

Morgan, Gareth. *Riding the Waves of Change: Developing Managerial Competencies for a Turbulent World.* San Francisco: Jossey-Bass, 1988.

Muller, Robert. *New Genesis: Shaping a Global Spirituality.* Garden City, NY: Doubleday and Company, 1984.

Mumford, Jonn. *A Chakra & Kundalini Workbook: Psycho-Spiritual Techniques for Health, Rejuvenation, Psychic Powers & Spiritual Realization.* St. Paul, MN: Llewellyn Publications, 1994.

Nair, Keshavan. *A Higher Standard of Leadership: Lessons from the Life of Gandhi.* San Francisco, CA: Berrett-Koehler, 1994.

*Ornstein, Robert, and Paul Ehrlich. *New World New Mind: Moving Toward Conscious Evolution.* New York: Doubleday, 1989.

Pearson, Carol S. *The Hero Within: Six Archetypes We Live By.* San Francisco, CA: Harper & Row, 1989.

Peat, F. David. *Lighting the Seventh Fire: The Spiritual Ways, Healing, and Science of the Native American.* New York: Carol Publishing Group, 1994.

Peck, M. Scott. *A Different Drum: Community Making and Peace.* New York: Simon & Schuster, 1987.

_____. *A World Waiting to Be Born: Civility Rediscovered.* New York: Bantam Books, 1993.

Phegan, Barry. *Developing Your Company Culture: The Joy of Leadership*. Berkeley, CA: Context Press, 1994.

*Power, Sally. "Mutually Uncommitted." *Business Ethics*, September /October 1995.

*Quinn, Daniel. *Ishmael*. New York: Bantam/Turner Books, 1993.

*Ransdell, Eric. "What's Black and White and Working?" *Fast Company*, Premier Issue, 1996.

Renesch, John, ed. *New Traditions in Business: Spirit and Leadership in the 21st Century*. San Francisco, CA: New Leaders Press, 1991.

Rhinesmith, Stephen H. *A Manager's Guide to Globalization: Six Keys to Success in a Changing World*. Burr Ridge, IL: Irwin Professional Publishing, 1993.

Rifkin, Jeremy. *Biosphere Politics: A New Consciousness for a New Century*. New York: Crown Publishers, 1991.

_____. *Time Wars: The Primary Conflict in Human History*. New York: Henry Holt and Company, 1987.

*Ross, Rick. "The Ladder of Inference," in Senge, Peter M., et. al., *The Fifth Discipline Fieldbook: Strategies and Tools for Building a Learning Organization*. New York: Doubleday Currency, 1994.

Roszak, Theodore, Mary E. Gomes, and Allen D. Kanner, eds. *Ecopsychology: Restoring the Earth, Healing the Mind*. San Francisco: Sierra Club Books, 1995.

Russell, Peter, and Roger Evans. *The Creative Manager: Finding Inner Vision and Wisdom in Uncertain Times*. San Francisco, CA: Jossey-Bass Publishers, 1992.

*_____. *The Global Brain: Speculations on the Evolutionary Leap to Planetary Consciousness*. Los Angeles, CA: J.P. Tarcher, Inc., 1983.

Russell, Peter. *The White Hole in Time: Our Future Evolution and the Meaning of Now*. San Francisco, CA: HarperSanFrancisco, 1992.

*"Saints and Sinners." *The Economist*, June 24, 1995.

Schaef, Anne Wilson, and Diane Fassel. *The Addictive Organization: Why We Overwork, Cover Up, Pick Up the Pieces, Please the Boss & Perpetuate Sick Organization*. San Francisco, CA: HarperSanFrancisco, 1990.

Schmidheiny, Stephan, with the Business Council for Sustainable Development. *Changing Course: A Global Business Perspective on Development and the Environment*. Cambridge, MA: MIT Press, 1992.

Schmookler, Andrew Bard. *Fool's Gold: The Fate of Values in a World of Goods.* San Francisco, CA: HarperSanFrancisco, 1993.

Schumacher, E.F. *A Guide for the Perplexed.* New York: Harper & Row, 1977.

_____. *Small Is Beautiful: Economics as if People Mattered.* New York: Harper & Row, 1973.

Schwartz, Peter. *The Art of the Long View: Planning for the Future in an Uncertain World.* New York: Doubleday Currency, 1991.

Schwarz, Jack. *The Path of Action.* New York: E.P. Dutton, 1977.

Seed, John, Joanna Macy, Pat Fleming, and Arne Naess. *Thinking Like a Mountain: Toward a Council of All Beings.* Philadelphia, PA: New Society Publishers, 1988.

*Senge, Peter M. *The Fifth Discipline: The Art & Practice of The Learning Organization.* New York: Doubleday Currency, 1990.

Seymour, John, and Herbert Girardet. *Blueprint for a Green Planet: Your Practical Guide to Restoring the World's Environment.* New York: Prentice Hall, 1987.

*Shipka, Barbara. "Beadwork." In Bill DeFoore and John Renesch, eds., *Rediscovering the Soul of Business: A Renaissance of Values.* San Francisco, CA: New Leaders Press, 1995.

*_____. "Corporate Poverty: Lessons from Refugee Camps." In Pat Barrentine, ed., *When the Canary Stops Singing: Women's Perspectives on Transforming Business.* San Francisco, CA: Berrett-Koehler, 1993.

*_____. "A Sacred Responsibility." In John Renesch, ed., *Leadership in a New Era: Visionary Approaches to the Biggest Crisis of Our Time.* San Francisco, CA: New Leaders Press, 1994.

*_____. "The Seventh Story: Extending Learning Organizations Far Beyond the Business." In Sarita Chawla and John Renesch, eds., *Learning Organizations: Developing Cultures for Tomorrow's Workplace.* Portland, OR: Productivity Press, 1995.

*_____. "Softstuff Application: Developing Work Teams in Technical Organizations." In Kazimierz Gozdz, ed., *Community Building: Renewing Spirit & Learning in Business.* San Francisco, CA: New Leaders Press, 1995.

*Shirer, William Lawrence. *Gandhi: A Memoir.* New York: Simon & Schuster, 1979.

Sieczka, Helmut G. *Chakra Breathing: Pathing to Energy, Harmony, and Self-Healing.* Mendocino, CA: LifeRhythm, 1994.

Spencer, Sabina A. and John D. Adams. *Life Changes: Growing Through Personal Transitions.* San Luis Obispo, CA: Impact Publishers, 1990.

Starhawk. *The Fifth Sacred Thing.* New York: Bantam Books, 1993.

*_____. *Truth or Dare: Encounters with Power, Authority, and Mystery.* San Francisco, CA: Harper & Row, 1987.

Storm, Hyemeyohsts. *Seven Arrows.* New York: Ballantine Books, 1972.

Tart, Charles T. *Open Mind, Discriminating Mind: Reflections on Human Possiblity.* San Francisco, CA: Harper & Row, 1989.

Theobald, Robert. *The Rapids of Change: Social Entrepreneurship in Turbulent Times.* Indianapolis, IN: Knowledge Systems, Inc., 1987.

Tichy, Noel M., and Mary Anne Devanna. *The Transformational Leader.* New York: John Wiley & Sons, 1990.

Trevelyan, George. *A Vision of the Aquarian Age: The Emerging Spiritual World View.* Walpole, NH: Stillpoint Publishing, 1984.

Trompenaars, Fons. *Riding the Waves of Culture: Understanding Diversity in Global Business.* Burr Ridge, IL: Irwin Professional Publishing, 1993.

Trungpa, Chogyam. *Shambhala: The Sacred Path of the Warrior.* Boulder, CO: Shambhala, 1984.

Vardey, Lucinda, comp. *Mother Theresa: A Simple Path.* New York: Ballantine Books, 1995.

Ventura, Michael. *Shadow Dancing in the USA.* Los Angeles, CA: Jeremy P. Tarcher, Inc., 1985.

*Vonnegut, Jr., Kurt. "Afterword." In *Free to Be...You and Me.* New York: McGraw-Hill, 1974.

*Wall, Steve, and Harvey Arden. *Wisdomkeepers: Meetings with Native American Spiritual Elders.* Hillsboro, OR: Beyond Words Publishing, Inc., 1990.

Walsh, Roger, and Frances Vaughan. *Paths Beyond Ego: The Transpersonal Vision.* Los Angeles: Jeremey Tarcher/Perigee, 1993.

**Webster's Ninth New Collegiate Dictionary.* Springfield, MA: Merriam-Webster, Inc., 1986.

Weil, Andrew. *Natural Health, Natural Medicine.* Boston, MA: Houghton Mifflin, 1995.

Weisbord, Marvin R., et al. *Discovering Common Ground: How Future Search Conferences Bring People Together to Achieve Breakthrough Innovation, Empowerment, Shared Vision, and Collaborative Action.* San Francisco, CA: Berrett-Koehler, 1992.

Weisbord, Marvin R. *Productive Workplaces: Organizing and Managing for Dignity, Meaning, and Community.* San Francisco, CA: Jossey-Bass, 1988.

Wheatley, Margaret J. *Leadership and the New Science: Learning about Organization from an Orderly Universe.* San Francisco: Berrett-Koehler, 1992.

*White, Frank. *The Overview Effect: Space Exploration and Human Evolution.* Boston, MA: Houghton Mifflin Company, 1987.

*Whyte, David. *The Heart Aroused: Poetry and the Preservation of Soul in Corporate America.* New York: Doubleday Currency, 1994.

*Williams, Margery. *The Velveteen Rabbit, or How Toys Become Real.* New York: Holt Rinehart and Winston, 1983.

Williams-Heller, Ann. *Kabbalah: Your Path to Inner Freedom.* Wheaton, IL: The Theosophical Publishing House, 1992.

*Williamson, Marianne. *A Return to Love.* New York: HarperCollins, 1992.

Wing, R.L. *The Tao of Power: Lao Tzu's Classic Guide to Leadership, Influence, and Excellence.* Garden City, NY: Doubleday/Dolphin, 1986.

Zuboff, Shoshana. *In the Age of the Smart Machine: The Future of Work and Power.* New York: Basic Books, Inc., 1984.

*Zukav, Gary. "Evolution and Business." In Michael Ray and Alan Rinzler, eds., *The New Paradigm in Business: Emerging Strategies for Leadership and Organizational Change.* Los Angeles, CA: Jeremy P. Tarcher/Perigee, 1993.

Index

Barbara Shipka's consulting practice, Willowheart, focuses primarily on creating a global orientation, building relationships and teams, working with diversity, and leveraging growth, change, and transitions. Among her clients are American Express, Cargill, Cray Research, Honeywell, Levi Strauss, Medtronic, and Pillsbury.

Ms. Shipka serves on the Board of Directors of The World Business Academy, initiated the Minnesota WBA Chapter, and is a member of the WBA *Perspectives on Business* and Global Change Editorial Committee. In addition to her work within the corporate sector in the United States, she has worked with the United Nations, non-governmental organizations, and in education in Europe, the Middle East, Africa, and the Caribbean.

Ms. Shipka is a contributing author to several anthologies on transforming business, including *The New Business of Business* (to be published in 1997) and *Rediscovering the Soul of Business.*

Barbara Shipka and her associates offer workshops, seminars, individual and organizational consultation related to leadership as a sacred journey. For more information, write: Willowheart, P.O. Box 50005, Minneapolis, MN 55405.